THE FOREST HOUSE

ALSO BY JOELLE FRASER

The Territory of Men: A Memoir

THE
FOREST
HOUSE

A Year's Journey Into the Landscape of Love, Loss, and Starting Over

Joelle Fraser

COUNTERPOINT
BERKELEY

The Forest House
Copyright © 2013 by Joelle Fraser

Library of Congress Cataloging-in-Publication Data
Fraser, Joelle.
  The forest house : a year's journey into the landscape of love, loss, and
starting over / Joelle Fraser.
      p. cm.
  ISBN 978-1-61902-113-6 (pbk.)
  1. Loss (Psychology) 2. Divorce. 3. Mothers and sons. I. Title.
  BF575.D35F73 2013
  818'.603—dc23   2012040586

Cover design by John Yates
Interior design by meganjonesdesign.com

Brush paintings copyright © Crystal Keesey
www.crystalkeesey.com

COUNTERPOINT
1919 Fifth Street
Berkeley, CA 94710
www.counterpointpress.com

Printed in the United States of America
Distributed by Publishers Group West

10 9 8 7 6 5 4 3 2 1

To children everywhere, and the parents who love them

AUTHOR'S NOTE

The Forest House *takes place between February 2010 and February 2011. Many names and identifying features have been changed in the interest of privacy. What remains is my story, and mine alone. As always, others have their own stories to tell. In the writing of this book, I have tried hard to remember, and respect, the difference.*

CONTENTS

CHAPTER 1

The Forest House

In Spanish, sierra nevada *means "snowy mountain range," an appropriate name because the Sierra is one of the snowiest places in North America. Only the coastal ranges of the Pacific Northwest, from Oregon to Alaska, regularly receive greater snowfall than the Sierra.*

— STEPHEN WHITNEY, *A SIERRA CLUB NATURALIST'S GUIDE TO THE SIERRA NEVADA*

I MOVED TO THE forest house in the last days of January, when the wind sailed down from the Sierra, and snow fell in long, blinding sheets that knocked out power lines, plunging our small town into darkness and freezing the streets in layers of ice. When my husband was at work, and the roads safe enough, I drove the eight winding miles back and forth from the small town of Susanville with suitcases full of clothes, boxes of books and toys, dishes and blankets, and whatever caught my eye as necessary for a new life.

1

Often I was the only car on the road, and aside from the cattle strewn across the icy meadows of Palmer Ranch, and the few horses pastured along the way, there were few signs of life. Through this winter landscape I drove as if partly submerged, staying one breath ahead of the fear, and guilt. My thoughts were occupied with the immediate and the pressing, as I was aware only that I had a few days to make a home for my son and me.

We were moving to a beautiful but slightly dangerous place, a tiny one-bedroom house on ninety-seven wooded acres at the end of Diamond Fall Road, at the county line, just before the pavement ends and the road turns to dirt and tunnels into the trees. The driveway is a steep, narrow dirt road, a quarter mile long, with two doglegs on the way up. Like the few other houses out this way, mine is hidden, much like a little nest, in the forest that begins here and continues for hundreds of miles into the mountain ranges of the northern Sierras and southern Cascades. I felt this to be truly the edge of the world I knew.

In my state of mind, driving to my new home was thus an odd act of faith: I never could see it until I was almost to the door itself.

Sometimes, when I wasn't fast enough to beat the weather, flakes of snow would begin to drift down from the sky, obscuring my tracks both behind and ahead, the evidence of my coming and going, and I would feel an otherworldly sense of being neither here nor there, but always *in between*. It was not just about moving from one place to another, but moving from one part of myself to another. This surreal feeling exhilarated me, but it was frightening, too. It was in those times that I questioned my choice to live so far from town. But by then, it already seemed too late.

Besides, the solitary location appealed to me—first because of my own quiet, private nature, but also because of the circumstances. There was the practical matter of the unbeatable rent: $400 for a cozy (if old and cranky) house on nearly a hundred acres. Though other towns might have offered options, and been a better fit for me, the nearest was eighty miles away, on roads often impassable in winter. To go so far afield would make it too hard for my child, who, I was determined, would always live close to his father.

The location drew me too because divorce is a sad, shameful thing—there's no getting around it—and in such a small, conservative town as the one in which we live, privacy would offer at least a temporary reprieve from the surprise and dismay that, like a rising tide, was coming our way once news got out.

Most of all, there was something I'd lost as my marriage crumbled, slowly and inexorably as a shallow, poorly built wall. I sensed, in the way you sense the inevitable, such as the way you feel the day's shift to night, that I couldn't find what was lost or heal what was broken in a place of noise and neighbors and the rhythms of ordinary life.

In many ways, the forest house was almost too good to be true, and without it I would not have had the strength to leave.

ASIDE FROM THE terrible emotions, I'd never gone through a more difficult move. Because the house had been vacant for months, the

last stretch hadn't been plowed since before Christmas, when the
landlord came to check on the pipes. So, more than once, after a
fresh snowfall my car wouldn't make it up the final steep curve, and
I'd park halfway up and trek the last hundred yards. Those days, I
made as many trips as my legs could manage, huffing and puffing
through snow to my knees with a lamp or load of toys, Dorfy the
dinosaur peering at me over the edge of the box, his tiny jaws gap-
ing wide in what—disbelief? Outrage? Some kind of crazed glee?

I could have waited for the convenience of spring to move,
for its warmth and lift. Winter is a terrible time to move, to make
dramatic changes, most of all to end a marriage. And if you live
in a forest, winter is a season to prepare for in the autumn, and
even—if you have a fireplace—in the summer. I was out of my
element. A good part of my life I'd actually lived in the tropics, in
Hawaii. Even here in the high desert of northeast California, with
its harsh winters, I'd always lived in a conveniently heated house
in town, two blocks from Main Street and Susanville Supermarket,
with neighbors close enough to have conversations through our
open windows.

I could have waited, too, until I'd squirreled away more
money, found some decent pieces of furniture, set aside a matching
set of dishes—waited for yet more confirmation that I was doing
the right thing. We'd been unhappy for so long, for years; why not
stay a little longer? All I can say is that I was dying a little more
every day, and that finally I had no choice any longer—ready or
not, snow or no snow.

Into the unheated house, my breath trailing in the air, I brought and set things along the empty walls. As far as I could tell, the only difference in temperature between inside and outside was the wind chill. But how I loved this place! A fireplace anchors the large living room, which is separated from the kitchen by a small bar, with room for two stools. The kitchen, a tiny u-shaped space, allows just enough room for one cook. I can stand in there and easily, at the same time, touch the counters on both sides; but because it overlooks the living room, the result is cozy rather than claustrophobic. A little window over the sink looks out onto the forest and the Diamond Mountains, which rise like a green cape seven thousand feet into the sky.

I decided to share the large bedroom—the only other room besides the bathroom—with my son, of whom I had fifty-fifty custody. I would divide it in half with bookshelves that form a kind of border between us. Eventually the two sides of the room would be decorated according to mom and boy.

The one strangely convenient feature of the house is the presence of a garage, with an electric door. It's ancient and moody, and it opens grudgingly with a mechanical, ear-cringing groan. But I knew that, once the driveway was plowed, the garage would keep the snow off the car, a fabulous benefit in winter.

After the electricity was turned on, just before we moved in, I brought up a little CD player. I'd put on Hawaiian music while unpacking each armload, the soft ukulele chords wondrous in the empty room. Sometimes I played Greg Brown, listening to his Iowa croon. It wasn't the words, but the tone beneath that I heard, the sense of longing and hope and loss. It made me laugh and cry and, once in a while, pause in the stillness to gaze around in silent astonishment at what I had done, and done myself.

Finally, after almost two weeks, I'd made a semblance of a home, something between a campsite and a motel room, with a small couch, kitchen table, a few chairs, and a mattress on the floor for me and a donated single bed for Dylan. To preserve the precarious truce with my husband, and to ease the transition for our son, I took as little as possible from the "town house," as Dylan began to call it. You'd never know a wife and mother had moved out. It was one of the many futile ways I tried to ease the fact of my leaving.

One morning I stepped outside to stack the pile of lodgepole pine and juniper delivered the day before. The porch looks out onto the Diamonds, and there's not a wire or a road or another house in sight. Just trees. As I breathed in the cold purity of snow on pine, it struck me: All those days of coming here, I hadn't seen anyone. Not people or animals or even birds. It was too deep in winter. This felt strangely right. I had, after all, decided to leave our unhappy marriage and live on my own; it felt necessary yet deeply awful, and I didn't want a witness. In the end, sometimes the only way to believe something is real is to go it alone.

That morning I became aware of the trees in a new way. They stood everywhere, narrow and tall, full and wide, an ocean of them spreading down the hill and up the face of the mountains in the distance. In that moment, I imagined each not as inert wood, but as a standing spirit, individual and present and alive. I became dizzy with the vision, the thousands of spirits surrounding me in all directions as far as I could see. Then, as if from some place both near and faraway, came the sound of wind in their branches. A soft chant, a whisper, and they said, *We are here.*

CHAPTER 2

The Dark Season

The Eurasian collared dove is a non-native species that has been able to adapt to many environments around the world, and across the United States, including the forests of California. The bird usually remains within close range of feeding and nesting sites.

Though not without predators, it can persist in harsh climates, including the snows of winter.

—U.S. FOREST SERVICE

W HEN I WAS young we often stayed the night in different places, and even when the circumstances were good—say we were visiting a family friend—I nearly always woke in the middle of the night with a terrifying sense of disorientation. It felt as if, in the quiet, strange-smelling dark, I was floating and utterly alone, weightless and transparent as a creature adrift in the ocean, with nothing to hold me to the world or to anything at all familiar.

There was no cure for the panic those nights, though I remember gripping bedcovers in my fists, and eventually I must have fallen back asleep. The remnants of this fear would shadow me throughout the next day, coloring even the ordinary moments. This happened so many times during my childhood that no single instance stands out: only a blurring unease—a thin black river coursing through my memories.

I fell into that river every night in those first months at the forest house.

IT'S STRANGE TO come to such a place and say, *This is where I live now, this is where I sleep and eat and wash my son's face and read his bedtime stories.* The house sets on the edge of a small town (pop. 7,800), which is itself burrowed high and away in an isolated area of northeast California, with the nearest city of Reno a two-hour drive. Geographically, this is a stunning place—the intersection of four ecological subregions—the Great Basin of Nevada, the Sierra Nevada, the southern Cascades, and the Modoc Plateau. The main feature though, for me, is a sense of being far, far away—at the edge of the world.

As a young woman I moved many times to apartments, city blocks, suburban streets. Even in the first days and weeks, when I knew no one at all, the movement of neighbors always presented a kind of normalcy in the midst of new surroundings, a familiar buffer against the unknown.

This is different. There is just the sky and the trees and the mountains. If I decided one day to step outside my door, I could easily slip into the forest and walk unseen for days and, eventually, disappear.

BECAUSE MY HOUSE is out of the way, and hard to find, no one ever just drops by. One friend became utterly lost, ending up halfway up the Diamond Mountains with her Honda's front end buried in a snowbank. She sent a text message because although the phone reception is bad, texts get through now and then. *WHERE ARE YOU??!* she wrote. It's as if a moat surrounds me.

"I don't know how you did it," more than one person has remarked. "And with such a small child, too." My aunt Kathy came for a visit in late March. A windstorm slammed through one night.

"Kathy," I said. "You've got to feel this. Come out on the porch."

We stood there together, bracing ourselves against the wind sweeping down from the Sierras that travel the backbone of northeast California, smelling of pine and moss and deep snow. Gusts rushed at us like swift, fierce animals. Our clothes billowed, and our hair whipped our faces. We watched the trees bend at their waists, and I thought of the strong women of my family—my mother and grandmother and great-grandmother, and how much more I should draw on that strength.

"My God," my aunt said, and I thrilled at the admiration in her voice. "You stayed here alone this winter?"

"This is nothing." It was true. I told her about a night in February, when I lay in bed with chest pounding, listening as shock waves of gusting wind crashed into the house, one after another after another. It's during the storms that I imagine the forest is transformed into a tortured ocean, the mountains into enormous waves, and our house is riding up the face of one of those waves, on the verge of toppling into the narrow valley far below obscured in a green froth of trees; on those nights, it wouldn't have surprised me to wake in the morning fifty miles from here, with our house moored in the vast playa of Nevada's Black Rock Desert.

That February storm was particularly violent. Around three in the morning the wind downed a power line. The heater went out, and the little blue night-light, and almost at once the cold crept into the blackness of the room. I got up to make a fire, bringing in logs from the porch as fast as I could, fleece pajamas flapping and icy air stealing into the room every time I opened the door. I closed off the bedroom and bundled sleeping Dylan onto the futon couch with me in the living room. Until dawn I lay awake, listening to the crack of the sap in the fire, the blasts of wind against the windows, my son's soft snores on the pillow beside me.

IN THE MORNING it was sleeting, and the power still out, which meant no phone. Then, because I couldn't manually release the rusty electric garage door so we could drive to town (so much for modern convenience), Dylan and I walked down the road in the freezing rain, holding hands and slipping in mud and snow, to find the nearest neighbor, and after introducing ourselves, ask for help.

What stays with me more than the fear of the storm is the way Dylan slept through the night. Our three cats had joined us, and I felt like a caterpillar in a cocoon of bodies and blankets, safe for a while, not so much unable but unwilling to move.

THINGS TO DO before next winter:

- teach as many summer school classes as possible
- learn to put on chains
- buy a tool kit
- buy manual phone for when power goes out
- order 3 cords of wood
- get pepper spray
- buy giant flashlight, batteries, and emergency candles
- weatherize windows
- stock up on fleece, and the thickest socks ever made

Almost every woman asks me, "Aren't you afraid up there? You live *in the woods.* You should have a dog. For your walks. For protection."

No, I say, I have the cats. I rescued them all from horrible lives, and they repay me with reassurance. Cleo, who was barely existing under a building at the college where I teach English part-time, is a black-and-white "tuxedo" cat, small and squattish, with short legs and stunted tail. She looks like an oversized kitten, but her white whiskers and eyebrow hairs sprout wildly as an old man's. Max and Rosie— brother and sister—are coal black, long and languid as miniature panthers, with sensuous whiplike tails. Bounding through the snow, they bring to mind black musical notes skipping across a white page.

One afternoon a friend came to visit and brought her shepherd mix. The dog's energy bowled me over. It was like a giant mosquito had alighted on the porch. The cats and I take each other in small doses, these cozy pillows who come to life a few times a day. And then there is this: a dog is ever-fixated on the human, but a cat is all about self-preservation, and so makes for a better lookout. "Save yourself" is their motto; if they sense danger, they bolt and, unlike dogs, don't look back to see if you're coming. They're aware of every little thing. A car on Diamond Fall Road, half a mile away. The distant rumble of a tractor on Palmer Ranch, the echo of a coyote's bark. The steady path of a spider (bugs don't stand a chance here). I watch the cats to learn what's happening in our world, and to prepare for it.

When they're relaxed, so am I.

KEEPING BUSY KEEPS fear at bay. I stack wood, shovel snow, assemble furniture from neatly packaged boxes. The guy at World Market said the desk was a cinch—an Allen wrench was all I needed!—but I put the legs on wrong, the bolts jutting out in Frankenstein fashion, the desk wobbly as a short, fat man in heels.

"This isn't right," I told Dylan. He frowned and stepped back as the desk swayed four inches to the right. "What's wrong, Mama?"

"Mama doesn't know how to fix things."

Fuming, I propped a chair against the desk so it wouldn't fall over, thinking of my girlfriend who changes her own oil, and another who recently retiled her bathroom. I'm the type who misses Oregon because they pump your gas for you. I've always been dependent on others, mostly men, to take care of the practical things. Two days later, sitting at the kitchen table and staring at the useless desk, it came to me in startling clarity: The legs needed to fit on the opposite way.

When I worry about next winter, I think of the emigrants who, in 1849, journeyed not far from here on their way to California to make a new life. With ropes and starving oxen, they hauled their wagons up rock-strewn ravines; they slept clutching starving children to their chests in the kind of snowstorms that I watch through my windows. And my own Swedish ancestors, whom I'd only begun to learn about, had endured things I couldn't even imagine.

"Yes, but it's all relative," my friend, who lives in a tidy neighborhood in town, tells me. "You literally get snowed in up there. And you bring up your own drinking water and haul your garbage to town—that's so pioneer."

Not even close, I think. Aside from the power outages, I have electricity, hot water. If I read by candlelight it's by choice. Yet it's true that I'm extremely alone, at least when my son's not with me, and that I do live an unusual life, far from town and alone in the quiet forest.

This is the choice: to fear something or to look for its gifts. The quiet here, for example, can be like warmth, or air: Unseen, it fills the room and somehow keeps you alive. At times the silence is so total I can hear the little thumps of cat paws crossing the carpet.

Within the quiet, there is movement. I learn that stillness is an illusion. Later, when the snow melts, even on windless days every stalk of grass will be in motion, however slight, as if moved by breath. And when all seems at rest, then comes the swift swipe of a blue jay's descent, a blue stroke of a paintbrush across the view. The mountain this morning was awash in strips of fog that moved in the high breeze, like a woman unveiling herself.

Living here makes me aware of gentle change, something I haven't ever paid much attention to.

What should I be afraid of? Mountain lions, rattlesnakes, black bears, ax murderers? These have already been mentioned. More likely: the car stuck in snow on a black night; breaking a leg on my way down to the creek; and, God forbid, Dylan getting injured. There is no next-door neighbor, no ambulance close by. Twenty minutes at best—in good weather.

Then there are the other, intangible fears: bills, job security, actually being a single mother.

Still, what scares me most is that well of time late at night, and what the darkness allows to enter—the unchartable future and whether I have the strength to survive it. No longer am I the child wondering who will keep me safe. Now it's my job. This is what it means to be alone: I have to be strong, and keep my son happy and safe. I have to keep this wonderful roof over our heads.

CHAPTER 3

How to Leave

In almost every case involving an "orphaned" fawn, people misguidedly tried to help fawns that were not truly orphaned. Does leave their fawns unattended for several hours at a time. However, the doe is nearby, even if she is out of sight.

—CALIFORNIA DEPARTMENT OF NATURAL RESOURCES

FOR MONTHS I live on the edge of despair. I'm not prepared for the consequence of joint custody, of the loss of my son, the forfeiting of half his life. I had to make this devastating choice, sit with the crippling guilt of being the one who left. I miss the nurturing the most, the bedtime and morning time, the blurry face and tufted hair, the buttery warmth of just-left blankets. I thought I'd have these quiet, solitary mornings when he was grown, when I was old. I looked forward to them. Now I have them half of my life, and it's too much.

Though it is wonderful consolation that Dylan's father is devoted and I don't need to worry, the despair remains, the pang of waking to silence, to the sight of my son's empty bed.

How could I have known? After her husband's death, Joan Didion writes in *The Year of Magical Thinking* that we cannot know "ahead of the fact (and here lies the heart of the difference between grief as we imagine it and grief as it is) the unending absence that follows, the void, the very opposite of meaning, the relentless succession of moments during which we will confront the experience of meaninglessness itself."

Didion was writing of death, but isn't this loss of time with my child a kind of death? And will it ever end? In her memoir *Around the House and in the Garden*, Dominique Browning confesses to being racked with loneliness when her sons are with her ex-husband. "I'm feeling the pain of their absence . . . as sharply as if the divorce had just begun, as if I hadn't been on this schedule of separation and reunion for years. I will never adjust any more than I have . . ."

SYNONYMS FOR *ABSENCE*: removed, gone, missing, unavailable, unaccounted for, lost.

YOU SURVIVE BY setting a course. My great-grandmother taught me this, though she's been gone thirty years. Because she's gone, I look to her story, which has sustained me on many cold nights.

Her name was Emma, and on a November day in 1919, in Sweden, she lost all six of her children. In order to save them she had to leave them and emigrate to America. Though she couldn't have known it at the time, only four would follow when they were still children. The oldest stayed in Sweden until she was grown and married. The youngest, Karolina, never left. By the time Emma earned enough money to send for her, Karolina was four, and had lived with her foster family for two years, and had little, if any, memory of her own mother.

Why did my great-grandmother leave them? What could bring a woman to leave her family, her upper-class home, her country, and go to a foreign land to work like a slave, a land where she knew only a handful of words? Suddenly, because I did not know how to live without my son for even one night, it became very important that I understand. I knew almost nothing, did not even have her name right. When I told some of my relatives of my plans to learn about "Elsa," my uncle said—and I felt the shock of shame—"Emma. Her name was Emma."

Of course there was a story, one that's been with me always, fragments told from family gatherings; it was a remote but integral knowledge, much as the working of my unconscious body. We breathe, but how often do we pause to feel the air travel into our chest and through us?

I had only these hard facts: During the first World War, in a Swedish village, an arranged marriage that turned bitter. Six children in ten years. A failing business in wartime. Then, in 1919,

something terrible causes my great-grandfather to flee to America
to avoid prison. Emma follows months later, while the children are
separated from each other and sent to foster families and friends. It's
in America that Emma and Olaus finally divorce. A family undone.

I BEGIN TO collect stories and books and photographs, though
no one in the family knows much of what actually happened. My
grandmother and her sisters were too young to remember anything
much but impressions, and they shared only a few of these with
their children, which include my mother. I discover there is an oral
history of the second oldest daughter, my great-aunt Linea. In it
she tells of riding a sleigh to church on Christmas morning. From
her memory, this I imagine: Emma sits beside my great-grandfather
Olaus, who drives the sleigh, clasping the reins in his worn leather
gloves. The horse is draped in little tinkling bells and from beneath
comes the creaking of the runners.

Olaus turns to her and laughs, sweet liquor on his breath, for
he was always thirsty for alcohol. Motionless branches sail overhead. The girls huddle behind them in their shawls and blankets,
wearing Christmas dresses, their cheeks bright spots of rose. Emma
bundles newborn Karolina to her chest, so warm and alive, like
a second heart pulsing against her own—and there is no place in
heaven or earth to even imagine that in two years' time, she will
have to give this child away.

Like a boat they surge through snowdrifts lit by candelabras
in the windows of the cottages they pass. They're on their way to

church, rushing along the snowy path, though not even prayer can save them anymore.

A STORY TAKES shape. It began with the arranged marriage. Emma was to marry the butcher's son, Olaus Olson. The marriage would profit both families. I have my great-grandparents' wedding photo, taken in 1909, and they're beautiful in beautiful formal clothes, but they bear the stoic faces of the early days of photography subjects. I wonder if their expressions are less about the shutter speed and more about the grave predicament they found themselves in. She was nineteen—and still in love with a boy she'd met three years before; my great-grandfather was twenty.

Looking at the photo is like looking at a window that will shatter one day, but there's no sign of how precisely the pieces will break, into what patterns they will appear, or where the shards will fall. The shattering will not happen for another decade, and it will come in the form of an act of violence one autumn night. It was as if, that day, they looked not on the camera lens, but on the inevitable future before them. Did they know even then they were doomed?

EMMA LOST THEM all at once—six children, her beloved father, her home. They call the homeland the Mother Country; this she left too. But losing the children would capsize her. All of the tending would be gone. The braiding of hair and mending of the clothes. When a woman loses her children she loses the tasks that make up the better part of a day. You lose what you do and also who you are. In coming to America, where she found work as a domestic, Emma left the needs of her home and family, and instead took on those of another.

I think about my great-grandmother all the time. There's something she can teach me. The Swedish writer Marianne Fredriksson calls it the "forgotten," the knowledge of our ancestors that still exists within us—the emotional counterpart to the cast of our cheekbones, or the set of our shoulders. It's the instinctive way we respond to a sudden change in fortune, or to the many variations of loss.

The writer Wendell Berry describes this as "the profound and mysterious knowledge that is inherited, handed down in memories and names and gestures and feelings, and in tones and inflections of voice."

WHEN IT'S DYLAN'S time to be with his father, this is how I leave him at the end of the day:

1. Make sure he's not hungry or thirsty.
2. Find a little surprise to occupy him, so he won't be so aware of my going. A toy from the dollar store, a picture book picked up at a yard sale. A new, invented game he can play with his father.

3. Prepare him. At least thirty minutes before leaving, say, "I'm going to work when Papa gets home" (because he won't stand for my going to the forest house alone, without him). "Everybody goes to work," I tell him. He can understand this much, at least to a point. He's learning about inevitability.

4. Do not cry. Maintain a cheerful tone.

5. Tell myself he'll be fine as soon as I'm gone. Know that, to get myself together again, I will have to pull over on the way home. Think about the glass of wine I will drink in order to sleep. Pick someone to call if and when it gets very bad.

6. Forgive my husband for blaming me. Know that he's lost half of his son's life too. Try again to forgive myself.

No matter what I do, almost always, Dylan pleads, "Stay with me a little bit while longer, Mama. A tiny while." Then he'll put two fingers close together to show that he's not asking for very much after all, that can I please not go just yet. "Okay," I tell him. "A little bit while." This can go on for a long time. Finally he's willing to let me go with a kiss. "I'm off to work," I say. And the half-truth shames my spirit because I'm not going to work, though I have papers to grade and chores to do—I am going to the forest house, alone, without him, exactly what he doesn't want.

THE GOOD-BYES, DID they happen one by one? Maybe Emma said good-bye first to this child after the afternoon nap, and to another child a last good night as she's delivered to a family on the edge of the lake, and did she help settle that daughter into her new room (so strange because the girl would have a room to herself for the first time in her life), and did Emma whisper, *This is where you will sleep until I see you again?* All the while knowing that day would be many months, even years, in the future.

Who could endure that pain, again and again, six times over, repeating the same words, *I love you, we will be together again, be good.* Some might cry and others rage at her, another shrinks away. No, better not to know each girl's special fears, and the unique scent of her neck and curve of her cheek—because then each leaving would create a memory with its own distinct qualities of pain, each memory in turn needing to be attended to in a differ-ent way, weaving the weight into a loss that much more compli-cated, and harder to bear.

So, do it all at once. In a gathering, maybe, one morning in the kitchen, or during a warm lull in the warmest part of the after-noon—or, better still, at the train station, so that the excitement of the crowd and the noise present a distraction from the terror that flutters around them all. As always when the girls were together and a difficult task at hand, I imagine Emma's manner was strong but not severe—and so even in the horror of the separation, the girls were given reassurance and a lesson amid the disaster: *This must be done. Tears won't help. It will be all right.*

In such a gathering the impression would be of so many reaching arms and grasping fingers pulling at her skirts, and warm heads pressed against her knees and hips and the tallest to her shoulder, the whole of these children blended together. The leaving would thus be all at once and total, and the tearing away done in one final heave, like a ship's fierce laboring push from the dock and into the current of the sea.

CHAPTER 4

Comings and Goings

A bat entering a cave for the first time cannot know beforehand if the temperatures within will be suitable to maintain a positive energy until the end of winter . . . However, if the animal ends up surviving, then conditions were suitable . . . and the bat's survivors will likely return to that site the next winter.

—BERND HEINRICH, WINTER WORLD

S OMETIMES, THE SILENCE gets the better of me, and I wander down to Jack and Carla's place. They live a ways down the road, and if I cut through the forest I can enter through the back of their property. They're on the verge of retirement, but for now, Jack's a contractor, and Carla spends most of her time taking care of their animals—the koi in the fish pond, four dogs, and a boatload of cats. She's been a cat rescuer all her life. Together, Jack and Carla have built something spectacular.

When they bought their house ten years ago, Carla had at least a dozen cats, all victims of abuse, abandonment, even dog mauling. She put out little cat shelters, but after losing several cats (some run over, some disappeared), she wanted them safe in the house at night. Here at the end of Diamond Fall Road, we're firmly in the forest, and it teems with wildlife: bobcats, gray foxes, raccoons, owls, the occasional mountain lion or even black bear.

For months she got up at all hours, calling for the last two or three not yet accounted for. In the meantime, more desperate cats ended up with her, including two kittens thrown from a car at the bottom of her drive. Her cats now numbered nineteen.

"I lost so much sleep," she told me. "It was terrible."

Jack, tired himself, built her what friends call the Cat Taj Mahal, a cat shelter so incredible that she actually gives informal tours of it. It has three "rooms": The first is a large, converted shed with a heated sleeping area, and three tiers of shelves and individual beds for the cats. If you come in during naptime you'll see floor-to-ceiling cats nestled in rows of round beds—sort of like a cat library. Jack built the next room from the ground up, including pouring a concrete slab, with mesh fencing for the walls and a ten-foot ceiling. This enclosure, the size of my living room, is stocked with "cat trees" and carpeted shelves. Two real logs, dragged from the forest, slope diagonally from floor to ceiling for an authentic climbing experience. An electric water bowl runs continuously, filling the air with the pleasant sounds of a babbling brook.

Then, because Carla couldn't deny the cats grass to roll on, Jack built another enclosure, connected by a cat tunnel. Grass is planted for the floor, and catnip grows around the room's perimeter. Jack's project has earned him the Most Amazing Husband award among Carla's friends. A mutual friend, grieving her divorce, came back shaken from a conversation with him.

"He just loves Carla so much," she said to me. "You can see it in his eyes, the way he talks about her. He built that so she could be at peace. I never felt that kind of love. I'm fifty-three and I've never felt that."

DYLAN IS ENCHANTED with the forest house and seems to adjust to the schedule, but I wonder if my cats are happy about our move from their small fenced yard. There was much more action in our neighborhood. Dogs, delivery trucks, kids shouting, a bigger house and more voices to fill it. My husband hated the cats, though, so there was that.

Here, there's no one else. It's so hidden in the trees that, if the temperature were about forty degrees higher, you could stride out onto the porch stark naked and dance like a crazy person. No one would see or hear. The actual sound of a human voice, even one carried by a faraway wind, makes us all stop and listen in surprise.

"Mama," Dylan will say. "Who *was* that?"

This utter privacy means that when your child is at his dad's, you can absolutely fall apart, collapse to your knees and sob until your lungs catch on fire, and no one will ever know.

"YOU CAN ONLY have three cats," my stepmom Kaui told me after she opened her email and saw the picture of Rosie, Max, and Cleo sitting side by side on the couch, like three enormous mushrooms. I don't remember her ever owning any kind of pet, not even a fish. For her, three cats in a one-bedroom residence is a sign of potential ruin. She's neat and stylish, with a razor-sharp sense of decorum, and I've not forgotten a comment she made a long time ago, when I was setting up my dorm at college: "A lady always has a bottle of good champagne in the fridge, just in case."

I used to be a one-cat woman. I had Oshkosh for most of my childhood, took a break during college and grad school, then adopted John Denver, a gray tabby who'd been rescued on a sweltering day from a pack of mischievous boys. He kept me company through six tumultuous years before he disappeared one day, just before Dylan was born. I still have a framed picture of John, sitting demurely beside a vase of red roses, that will never be put away.

Then something happened while I was married and a new mother. I began to notice, and dwell on, the poor predicaments of the animals in the neighborhoods. This is a hunting, ranching town: In general, animals are viewed as tools, targets, and/or dinner. As far as cats and dogs go, our animal shelter overflows with the unwanted. I slowly got involved with the local Humane Society by writing a pet column for our weekly paper. Now and then, I help trap and transport ferals to be spayed and neutered.

In this town especially, my volunteer work is considered a little odd, even misguided. Why not spend that energy on helping people? To which I say, it's all connected, and besides, who can tell another how to love? The brilliant poet Mark Doty, when chastised for his dream of opening a shelter for homeless retrievers instead of giving shelter to people, wrote in his memoir *Dog Years*:

> *It seems that compassion for animals is an excellent predictor of one's ability to care for one's fellow human beings.*
>
> *But the plain truth is no one should have to defend what he loves. If I decide to become one of those dotty old people who live alone with six beagles, who on earth is harmed by the extremity of my affections? There is little enough devotion in the world that we should be glad for it in whatever form it appears, and never mock it, or underestimate its depths.*

At least to my husband, my efforts were a colossal waste of time, so he ignored them. To keep the peace, I learned to keep quiet. This wasn't always possible, though, and a year ago, when several cats were abandoned three houses away, I took in two of them—Rosie and Max—despite the friction I knew it would cause.

MOST OF THE time my cats sleep in front of the fireplace, curled around each other sleek as seals in their round pet bed, which is a plaid brown with a giant paw print in the middle. When they're like this, there's no telling where one begins and the other ends.

They sleep, arms and tails braided. It's one of the most calming sights in Creation, these slumbering cats. It's like yoga for the eyes.

I'd have to agree with May Sarton, who wrote in *The House by the Sea* that "solitude shared with animals has a special quality and rarely turns into loneliness."

Then some mornings, like this one, I wake and find only two cats. Today it's the girls: Rosie and Cleo. Max is missing. I stoke the fire, make coffee, stand by the door, peer left and right. After a while I wander out to the porch, shivering in the cold, to look up and down the slope and call "Max! Here kitty kitty," hoping to see a black blur threading toward me. That's what usually happens. But the forest is quiet this morning. It's nearly nine o'clock. The thought comes, *It's finally happened*, and I imagine Max clamped in the foul-smelling jaws of a bobcat.

I go back inside to wait some more, and try to write. I hate this. But then, half an hour later, there he is. Nose to the door, wet with snowmelt. I open the door and in he strolls, straight to the food dish. I snatch him up and kiss him and hold him for a few moments, breathing in smells of pine and earth and last night's snow. He glances up, his expression almost a frown, as if he's thinking, *You worry too much*.

A therapist would probably say my cat-nurturing is a way of dealing with missing my son. Maybe so. In any case, by April, something had to change. Like Carla, I was fed up with trying to herd in the cats before going to bed, prowling in the freezing dark in my pajamas and unlaced snow boots, coaxing the last one inside.

"Okay," I'd say. "Now sleep through the night for once, will you?"

Cats never do. They're crepuscular rather than strictly nocturnal, meaning they're most active in the dim lighting at dawn and dusk. Which is why I was awakened every morning with the sun, and after letting them out, would try, mostly in vain, to go back to sleep.

So I ordered a cat door, wincing at the price. It's a marvelous invention—a glass panel that attaches to the sliding glass door, with a five-by-seven-inch opening at the bottom, secured with a magnetic flap that a cat pushes open with its nose. It took a few days for the cats to figure it out, and I have to say it's one of the top ten purchases I've made in my life. Many animal experts will say cats should stay indoors. It's safest. And yes, a fox or an owl might grab one of my cats one black night. But I've never been able to deny them the outdoors. Day and night, they come and go as they please. I love the sight of them chasing shadows, or loping down the hill behind the house, or poking in the dry grass beyond the porch, ears swiveling to each sound. How can I keep them from all that?

I KNOW THE cats are aware of my comings and goings too. When I return from leaving Dylan with his father, and I'm facing three nights alone, the cats keep me on track. As soon as I walk in the door they're sitting there, obviously just up from a nap. They yawn at me: *You can relax. All is well. Nothing dangerous here or around the house.*

Then they let me know it's dinnertime. I set out their bowls, freshen the water, fuss over them. I lean down to pick up each cat in turn, hearing them purr. I do this for a long while, until it feels true that yes, at least for now, I am home and all is well.

CHAPTER 5

You Get By

Ravens require that large carcasses are opened up, and so they follow packs of wolves or coyotes. Ravens are thrifty and regularly eat and recycle wolf scat. Moose kills and available big-game carcasses are limited and uncertain, and so ravens have learned how to weather lean times.

—Dr. Reese Halter, "Clever Ravens"

I DON'T LIKE TO call people late at night. That's when memoirs come to the rescue. I have a shelf full, gathered over the years, but in the past months have sought what I call "life memoirs," written by women. They tell stories about living through something—usually some kind of loss—and coming out the other side.

A large subset—"split-lit"—deals with divorce; what *The New York Times* calls "divorce porn." When I can't sleep, I voraciously read them while buried in blankets, one after another—consuming them like literary bonbons. Most of them are written by middle-aged women, but not all, and their wisdom and wry humor have sustained me on many a cold night.

After a while, I was struck by a commonality of these authors: They all seem to have money. Sometimes lots of money. To heal, they buy the best furniture they can find; they live in New York apartments, they vacation in summer beach houses, and travel to Italy to eat at sidewalk cafés. They own their own homes with sumptuous guest rooms; they call on architects and tend to flowering gardens, and their sheets have a thread count of six hundred. When they work, if they work at all, they produce television shows and write for high-paying, slick magazines.

So, it was about the time I applied for food stamps that I reluctantly put away this stack of memoirs. They would not help me with this part. Having spent years as a "stay-at-home" mom, I had just started teaching part-time at the college, earning a monthly paycheck of $850.00—no benefits. No full-time jobs were on the horizon for several years.

Like every other business, my husband's was hurt by the recession. Still, he will make sure Dylan is taken care of, even if he has to sell the shirt off his back. But what about me? Dealing with custody is enough for now; I leave finances alone. In the meantime, it seems prudent to take some precautions.

Which is why I was standing there in line at the welfare office, at the age of forty-three, with my three master's degrees under my tightened belt. Even though I didn't come from money—even calling us middle-class was always a small stretch—who could make sense of this picture for me? I've never done anything like this before, and few relatives have either. Sure, my aunt spent a few months on unemployment between jobs, and during a rough patch, my brother once ate Thanksgiving dinner at a Salvation Army kitchen. For the most part, although our family did a lot of bootstrap pulling, we always had boots.

Yet in some way I've been waiting for this to happen all of my life.

THIS IS A prison town. More people (over ten thousand) live behind bars than outside of them; half the town is made up by guard and inmate families. Partly because of these incarcerated men, and the families who've come to live here, the town is full of "people in need." I imagined the possibility of joining them. Hadn't I accepted handouts from a friend in my writing group? She brought up a single bed from her guest room, for my son. And a box of matching sheets.

My brother gave me a portable DVD player that his six-year-old daughter had outgrown. They used it for road trips, and the screen is about the size of a salad plate. I sit on the couch, watching movies borrowed from the library. A pinkie-sized Matt Damon–as–Jason Bourne leaps across the rooftops of Tangier. Even while I squint, there's something comforting about making do, about living within your means.

I've also begun to shop at Grocery Outlet, a place I'd never been to before. My mother calls it "Used Foods," with no scorn;

she loves the place. Now I go there regularly. You can get everything from toothpaste to T-shirts, oranges to Ovaltine, at rock-
bottom prices. Happily, they've got tons of organic products. Most
of the items are overstock, and some are close to the expiration
date, or a bit beaten up. You have to be careful.

Other cruiseworthy places include Nu 2 U, the Dollar Tree
aisles, and Walmart, where I push Dylan along in the shopping
cart. Everything is so bright! For a tiny town, we have quite a few
businesses dedicated to cheap prices, and what else can you do but
be grateful?

INTENSE CHILDHOOD MEMORIES never really fade. I can't forget
the outraged dismay that overcame my fourteen-year-old self when
I discovered someone had stolen my clothes from the dryer at the
Coast Laundromat in Lincoln City, Oregon. Oh, how I'd saved for
those precious pairs of brand-name jeans! So many, many hours
vacuuming sand and pubic hair from the rooms of the Surfrider
motel, where I worked after school as a maid. All my life—except
when I was married—there never seemed to be enough money,
enough anything.

YEARS LATER, WHILE in graduate school in Iowa, I cleaned the
kitchen and bathrooms of the rooming house I lived in. One day

a fellow student—most of the writing program students were wealthy, it seemed—saw me coming around the corner with a mop and said with an exasperated frown, "Are you still doing that?" As if it were an experiment, or some research I was gathering for a short story. I was too proud to admit that the $80 paid for most of my month's groceries.

Still, what a privilege to go to graduate school! I would leave with a degree that would enable me to teach college English classes. Now the best I can get in this small town is an adjunct position without benefits; adjunct, meaning subordinate, auxiliary, provisional. A part not essential to the whole.

THE WOMEN IN my family have always worked hard, and rarely had enough money. Emma, after a few years working as a maid in Michigan, finally made enough money to send for the first two of her daughters. They then reached Portland, Oregon, in 1924, where she found a job in the kitchen of the fancy Benson Hotel. She smuggled home eggs and blocks of butter in her bodice.

Her daughter Viola, my grandmother, worked as a maid and nanny, doing the most demeaning tasks. One that stands out to me as particularly horrible is the washing of the handkerchiefs—how she had to stir the cloths in a vat of boiling water, breathing in the foul steam while spooning out thick green globs of snot that rose to the top. Later she married my grandfather, a policeman, and worked as a bank teller. At home she gardened, cooked, cleaned, and sewed the clothes for their four children. Even when they retired comfortably, the fear of poverty, like an ever-present storm cloud, never lifted.

Once, as we finished our meal on a rare dinner out at a restaurant, I gaped at my grandfather as he offered the last half of his beer to the strangers at the next table. He didn't want it to go to waste.

"Uh . . . no thank you," stammered the man.

I'm glad my mother taught me to lighten up now and then. We were raised with the feeling of scarcity, yes, but not despair. She raised my brother and me alone, with no child support, let alone alimony. My aunts, and great-aunts, worked just as hard.

Each time I think of these women, my complaints and fears lessen. "You come from good stock," I was told time and again growing up. Let's hope so.

Now, while we wait for my caseworker, Dylan sits on my lap in front of the cutout window through which we'll be interviewed. We wait with all kinds of people—old grizzled men and pinch-faced women, young tattooed men with pants slung from their hips and babies in their arms, a woman in a wheelchair. No one smiles; untold damage all around.

Nobody knows we're here.

I try to do one of those out-of-body trips where you imagine yourself from a corner of the ceiling, looking down and observing yourself. Here is the picture: a nice-looking woman, with a cute child, sitting on plastic chairs on a scuffed floor. The woman offers the boy some whole grain crackers from a yellow snack container. She owns nothing but a twelve-year-old Honda.

Decent people! Nothing wrong here! But if you'd given me a crystal ball a few years ago and showed me this scene, I would have taken the ball and smashed it against a wall.

A FEW DAYS later, on a rare sunny afternoon, I was driving back from the college and saw a woman walking along the sidewalk in her socks. *What the hell?* I thought. Her steps were slow and careful, and her hair was flopping out of its ponytail, but otherwise she looked like a normal woman, maybe in her fifties. She had a sweet face, with large brown eyes. I had somewhere I was supposed to be, but turned around and asked her if she needed a ride.

For the next thirty minutes we drove from one place to another. I gave her my shoes—old ballet flats—and we went to her apartment. On the way she told me she'd walked from the hospital, where she'd spent the early morning hours after her boyfriend had knocked her in the head.

At her apartment she retrieved the key to her wheelchair, which she used when her bad back was out. We then drove to her wheelchair, which was parked in the middle of a weedy yard of an old house down the street. After settling herself into the chair, in which she resembled a forlorn child, she asked me to follow her home, because her boyfriend might be around, watching. I drove the six blocks at five miles per hour, behind her little rolling chair, back to her apartment, on the lookout for a lurking abusive monster.

"Is there anything else I can do?" I asked, as she pulled up beside my window.

"No," she said, shaking her head firmly. She thanked me several times, and we said good-bye. I drove off thinking, *You're alone now. If you're not careful, this is where you can end up: shoeless, tired, body collapsing one part at a time, and relying on a man who thinks he loves you with his fist.*

THE FOOD STAMP application went into the system, and myself with it. Who can foresee the future? That night I dreamed of my grandmother, and I woke remembering her hands, soft and gnarled as the driftwood she'd collected for her garden. All she endured, all her mother endured, and mine. What makes me think I'm any less of a woman? Of a survivor? If the application is denied I'll still have food to eat and a warm place to live and a job. You get by. And maybe, eventually, your life can be extraordinary.

Soon I began to read the memoirs again. One of the authors wrote of a friend who, in her forties, was still living with the "distinct staleness that comes with living too long like a college student: street-find furniture, plank-and-block bookcases." It wasn't lack of money, but waiting for true love that prevented her from finally buying her own house and gorgeously outfitting it.

I put down the book and spent a minute or two looking around at my thrift store furniture—the $2 bedside table, the scarred bookcase, the poster of a Hawaiian beach tacked on the closet door. So many items, bought out of necessity, not a mental block. Is it staleness around me? You might think so. But for me, these are just the practical choices of a careful woman who knows the edge is not so far away.

CHAPTER 6

Strange Country

After birth the young of the hoary bat cling tightly to the mother through the day, but are left clinging to a twig or leaf while she forages at night. The family generally occupies the same roost, but after disturbance the mother may move her babies to a new location.

—Roger W. Barbour and Wayne H. Davis, *Bats of America*

DYLAN IS MY compass. I orient myself to where he is at any given moment: at the park with his dad, at school, sleeping, riding his tricycle out on the porch. I check the clock: twelve fifteen, so he's halfway through lunch at preschool. I think of what's in his lunch box and imagine his smile when he sees I've packed his "Clifford the dog juice." With him, I no longer feel a little bit lost. Whatever else may be off-kilter—ants in the kitchen, another power outage, a bad night's sleep—as long as Dylan is next to me, I can navigate anything.

My mother once told me that when I had a child, I'd never be alone again.

She's right. Even when he's not with me, I'm alone with missing him. With his absence. A couple of years ago, when things weren't getting better, I saw a therapist in Reno. She recommended that parents separate before their children turn four. Any later, and the child may blame himself for the divorce, and may feel compelled to take care of his parents' emotions. This seemed sensible to me, but now I'm not so sure. At least not with true fifty-fifty custody. At such a young age, I believe a child needs his mother (no matter how loving his father) for more of the nurturing times—bed, bath, breakfast. I'm willing to admit my unfair bias, but still, the feeling haunts me, that Dylan needs me more, at this age.

My friends agree. They ask, "How do you get through it?" "Different ways," I say. Rent eye-popping action movies, take long, punishing walks and skin-scalding baths. Read affirmations and page-turners. Write until the ink runs out.

IT'S LATE MARCH, and the spring dawns wet and cold. Most nights a fire is necessary to take away the chill. I live day to day, not thinking much beyond the next time I'm with Dylan, or beyond the current batch of papers to grade. I teach basic writing through the correspondence office of the local college, bringing home stacks of envelopes filled with "unity paragraphs" and narrative essays and grammar exercises; most of my students are prison inmates, and their journal entries remind me to be grateful for what I have.

And summer is not so far away, after all, the days stretching longer. There's a makeshift routine now to our lives at the forest house, one that comforts when a bill arrives, or when my mother became ill enough to need an oxygen machine, or whenever an acquaintance—as happens often—inquires about my family, and I say "Fine, we're fine," which is an utter lie because we separated months ago and the divorce process is in full swing, and soon the whole town will know. But my husband—ever private—isn't ready to go public, and I respect his wishes. This deception, an ugly shadow, follows wherever I go.

My good friends know the situation, my "mom friends," I call them. They all have husbands and two or more children, and once upon a time we'd get together and talk about how to make our marriages better. Over coffee or cocktails, we vented, laughed, begged for advice. During the worst times, some of us even wondered aloud how it would be to go it alone. But it seemed impossible, insane even, to embark on the journey that ends with the end of a family. There came a day, though, when I felt I truly and literally had no choice anymore, knowing the needs in my marriage would be forever in conflict, and the cold civility that remained unbearable. The details are not important here. As the essayist Patricia Hampl writes, "What happens in the dark of human intimacy is holy, and belongs to silence. It is not, as we writers say, material."

So I broke for that strange country. From their fragile, familiar shores, my friends waved.

They get to visit. We had a few playdates at the forest house at first—it's easier for them to meet in town—where our kids ran wild. My friends checked out the house, saw the one bedroom divided in two, asked questions—*Will you ever be able to buy your own place? How will you get through the holidays? Do you ever get scared at night?* They listened with wary fascination when I told them it is harder than anything we ever imagined, and that I wouldn't wish my situation on anyone. And that, sometimes, I am so bewilderingly relieved that I have to sit down and say, *Yes, this is real.*

The particulars of my life amazed them, especially the idea of waking up alone, to silence that is never broken, not just once in a while, but for *several days in a row, every week.*

"It's so peaceful here," more than one friend commented. But theirs was a reluctant envy. "It must be nice," they said, and though their eyes were wistful, I could hear the doubt in their voices, like a faraway echo. To me, they always seemed glad to go home.

True joint custody, it seems, is still unusual. When my parents divorced in the 1960s, my mother raised me almost totally on her own. Two decades later my aunt, who shared custody of her son with his father, cared for Jake 80 percent of the time. These mothers are granted some sympathetic admiration, and rightly so. I may live paycheck to paycheck for the rest of my life, and never own my own home, but I will always be able to trust in and rely on Dylan's dad for our child's needs. That is an immeasurable blessing. And because Dylan is with his father three or four nights a week, I'm not harried and exhausted, but instead ever-patient and joyful with my child. It's taken me a long while to concede that benefit, darkly tainted though it is.

It's a peculiar thing to be a half-time mother, and painful in a way I can only describe as chronic. Dominique Browning is one of the few writers I've found who's had actual half-time with her sons. She never got used to it, calling joint custody "disjointed": "I have been going through the emptying of my nest on a pretty regular basis for years. Every week the children leave, on to their other nest, every week they return to mine."

It *is* disjointed. I didn't tell my friends about my coping ritual, about cleaning up the traces of Dylan's presence. The Little Tikes truck, the tiny farm set with its miniature chickens glued to a green plastic strip, the picture books wedged into the couch—these all disappear into his red toy basket. I make his bed, fold and put away the pile of pajamas (first breathing in their scent).

In the beginning I tried to leave his things where they lay, but the reminders were more painful. I kept expecting to see him sit down with his blocks, or ask me to read him a story. The house felt like a waiting place when he was gone, not a living place. So once a week, I put away the remnants of my child. In just minutes, the forest house— aside from our shared bedroom—looks like a single woman's place. Neat, tasteful, serene. It's an illusion of course, a mirage I inhabit, but even so, sometimes for long stretches, I can move forward.

For some, this splitting in half of a child's life is not worth it. I have one friend who plans to leave her unhappy marriage when her son, who is now seven, graduates from high school.

"That's twelve years from now," I point out. "You'll be, what, forty-eight?"

"Yep," she says.

This long-term plan of hers is what people mean when they say sacrifice. I begin to learn some of the nuance of guilt as I realize, these past months, that to some of my friends (and to most of this small, traditional town, for that matter), what I've done is selfish. *Okay*, I think. But at least I no longer have to hear the questions for which I had no answers—*What is happening to you? It's as if you've disappeared. Why are you so thin? Why don't you laugh anymore?* The worry in their eyes as I stir the pancake batter and say I just didn't sleep well, again.

I remember trying to make my mother happy. Can a child be content if his mother is not? If I free myself, do I free my son from carrying the burden of my unhappiness? It's too soon to tell, but that's what children do: They hold the weight of their parents' hearts.

For the first time in years, I can breathe deeply again. I'm gaining back the weight I'd lost so that my clothes don't hang off my bones anymore. I'm laughing again. And you haven't seen my son's beaming face when I get up to dance to Bob Marley or Tom Petty because, finally, I feel capable of dancing again.

"What are you doing, Mama?" he asked that first time.

"Dancing—I'm dancing."

"That's right, Mama," he said, and when I held out my hands, he came to join me.

ABIGAIL THOMAS WRITES of guilt in her memoir *A Three Dog Life*. Her husband had a traumatic brain injury, and it took her years to "hold these two truths in my head at once: I wish he were whole, and I love my life." I know what she means because I cannot even imagine saying, "I wish Dylan were with me all the time, and I love my life."

There is no win with divorce, not with kids, not that I can see. I agree with Barbara Kingsolver, who wrote that divorce is worse than being widowed: You lose the same things as the widow, but people don't gather to comfort you. There are some who can't believe you tried everything—that more counseling would have done the trick, or more prayer, or more anything. Others believe you have no right to be sad because you were the one who left, weren't you? What did you expect, really? Yet, divorce, Barbara Kingsolver writes with vivid accuracy, "is as much *fun* as amputating your own gangrenous leg."

How much worse with children? The hurt you didn't see coming. Dylan is with his dad on the weekends. Already Dylan has missed three of my friends' children's weekend birthdays. Still I tacked the invitations on my bulletin board, with their bright balloons and wide-eyed puppies, the shy pink princess. I imagined my friends with plates of cake on their knees, the shouts of children. They'd welcome me, but going without Dylan? Unthinkable. It's too awkward for my ex to go. Maybe one day these events can be negotiated, with Dylan's time traded and bartered, and those invitations swapped like playing cards. How do you make up for it all?

It makes me wonder about the geography of divorce—especially when you have young children—how its main quality is elusiveness. You get your bearings and then the boundaries change, mist obscures the path, plates shift, and the ground itself transforms into a foreign shape. What was hostile turns coldly polite; the accepted becomes debated. Where, in such nebulous territory, does the road lead? How, without a guide or map, can one prepare for it? What do you take with you on this journey—what do you leave behind? Hardest of all—your child has no choice but to travel this way as well.

It's this uncertainty that makes the forest house so important. In the landscape of divorce, one needs a refuge. For some it's family; my cousin moved into her mother's house for a few years. For others, work is the anchor. For me it's this house, and the trees and the mountains. And always, Dylan.

NAIVELY, I THOUGHT I'd get more calls and text messages and emails. Crystal calls once a week or so, but she's overwhelmed with graduate school and her four children. Only my best friend, who lives in Hawaii, checks in with me every other day or so. She sent me a book about ceremonies for important passages. Of course it makes sense that the friend who's stayed closest isn't married, and has no children. That's not to say she doesn't possess a brimming life, but there's something about children, at least when they're young, that intrudes on one's friendships. And I can't help suspecting that what I've done poses no threat to her sense of her herself.

My brother Ken, who also lives in Hawaii and is steadily married, suggested something else is at play: "It's like you have lung cancer. People feel really sorry for you—this terrible thing that's happened. But they also assume you've smoked most of your life, and so figure you're responsible for a big part of this. In their minds, it wouldn't have happened if you'd lived differently, made better choices, had stronger character. So they pity you, but they blame you too."

I wish I knew what my great-grandmother Emma did, after her marriage ended, after she had to give all six children away, not knowing when or even whether she would see them again. Did she save items from each child, pictures, locks of hair? When I think of her, and our family's history, I approach the sorrow from two sides—Emma's and her children's. One lost her children—the others, their mother.

When Emma left for America, my grandmother Viola, Emma's fifth child, was sent to live with a family friend in a nearby village. Viola was five years old then, and it was two years before her mother saved enough money for her ship passage. The friend was named Mama Ibee; she was the matriarch of a farming family, and Viola loved her. But she never stopped yearning for her mother.

My grandmother never spoke of her childhood to me, of Sweden or when she finally came to America at age seven. It could be I never asked. But one story she passed down to her children was also passed down to me; I've heard it so many times that it's hard to separate it from my own memories. The story is of a dream that followed her all her life: In that dream, my grandmother is standing on the grass at Mama Ibee's farm. Suddenly, her mother appears in the distance, coming toward her on a bicycle. But as soon as she gets close, Emma doesn't stop, just passes by, close enough that Viola can almost reach out and touch her mother's long black skirts billowing and flapping in the wind. Emma rides the bicycle in a large circle, around and around, faster and faster, each time passing by Viola and then rushing on with the *whoosh whoosh* of the wheels. The dream has no end, just the endless, circling mother with her long skirts like black, flying wings.

The dream haunts me. Maybe it reminds me of my own separation from my mother, when I was barely two years old. She was gone for a summer, and she left me in my grandmother's care. Did it comfort my grandmother to take care of me those months, or did it stir up the dark dream of her own vanished mother?

I know this much now: The sadness between mother and child is not the same. The grief between mother and child is shared, but not the same. I know what Viola maybe did not: The mother must also carry guilt.

One day in 1921, Emma received a letter from one of the foster families in Sweden. Her daughter Elsa, Viola's sister, had been with this family for two years; it was not a good situation, though this news would not come out until later.

As agreed, the foster mother had been sending letters telling of the progress of Elsa, who was now eight years old. Elsa got a hold of one of the letters before it was mailed and steamed open the flap. There she wrote: *Mama, come for me quick.* What did Emma think as she opened the letter and found her child's hidden handwriting? Her girl, Elsa, the third child with the clearest blue eyes and blond curls, whom she'd been told was happy. Did she think, *What have I done?*

I STILL MEET with my married friends, though not as often. We go to a coffee shop and order drinks with whipped cream. Our time is always rushed, though theirs seems more so, especially if their children are with them. Soon, they will have to leave, and they do, with gestures full of purpose and direction. The way is clear for them; they need no map. And, maybe later that night, they will fall into an exhausted sleep with the bittersweet satisfaction that only sacrifice can bring. I hold my cup and watch them wave as they drive away. I count the hours until I see my son again.

CHAPTER 7

Going Dark

Before the wood frog can freeze to death, the cells become packed with glucose . . . In about fifteen hours the frog is frozen solid except for the insides of its cells. Its heart stops. No more blood flows . . . By most definitions, it is dead. But it is prepared to again revive at a later date.

—Bernd Heinrich, *Winter World*

AFTER I TAKE Dylan to his father's, it's a dark drive to the forest house. Dark enough to need the bright setting of the headlights. How much easier it would have been to move later, when the days were long, when I could have driven home in the last of the light.

But the dark has taught me things. For one, when you live in the country, the way home is much different by day than by night. By day the way is clear. Even if the clouds have gathered on the Diamonds, I can still sense the slope of the mountains, their

immense arc and presence. Diamond Fall Road unravels before
me like a cast-off ribbon, and the cattle of Palmer Ranch arrange
themselves in never-ending patterns upon the meadow.

Then the forest begins and, like outliers, more and more pine
and oak appear, closing in on the road. It's less than a mile to home.

But in the country at night, the view disappears. No helpful
streetlights guide the path home, through neighborhood pools of
shadow. If you walk down my road after dark, better bring a flashlight. Context disappears too: the shape of the cottages down the
side roads, the familiar horses vanish inside fences and corrals, the
Appaloosa up on the hill invisible now as I round the fourth bend
of the road. They're gone from sight; I could be almost anywhere.

Perspective is gone as well on these dark drives. Lights in faraway windows transport this land into another century; now these
scattered houses become far-flung outposts of the old frontier. On
such drives home, for a while, I can lose myself.

But nothing—not even the radio—can silence the echo of
Dylan's words in my mind, that he wants me to stay. That he will
miss me. When I do leave, nothing can erase the image of my old
house in the rearview mirror, or the feeling that I've just left the
scene of a crime. What makes me think I can escape punishment by
listening to a song on the radio?

SOMETIMES I DO something crazy. It was a game we played as
teenagers, when I lived on the Oregon Coast. In Tillamook County,
long black miles of two-lane roads cut through dairy farm country

overshadowed by the Cascade Mountains. Some of these roads ran straight for quite a while, with no streetlights anywhere. Halfway down the road, whoever was driving would switch off the headlights: Instant, total, blackness. And the sensation of hurtling into it. There was always a second of shocked silence, then screams of terror, of hilarity, of madness. It was like rushing toward death.

The stupid things young people do. That was almost a lifetime away. Yet a few nights ago, on a stretch very much like that one so long ago, I turned off my headlights and flung myself into that blackness. The decision to do so reminded me of a line from a spy movie, when the main actor shuts down his communication lines and he's on his own—the last thing he said was, "I'm going dark."

How long were my headlights off? Three seconds at most. Afterward I pulled over to the side of the road to catch my breath, and in that great expanse of valley and mountain my car sat as tiny and unassuming as an extra button on a great flowing coat. I imagined Emma then on that ocean crossing from Sweden—how vast the watery landscape and how small her body lying in her berth. Imagined her on that vessel riding the slope of each endless, groaning wave. Her ship left in November, and how cold would the Atlantic have been? All her girls left behind—dispersed like young leaves pulled from their stems only to swirl, ceaselessly, on the surface of a cold lake.

THE OTHER DAY Dylan was leafing through a book and a picture fell out, one from a trip we took to Belize when he was nine
months old. I'm holding him in my arms, a round creamy cherub
in a swim diaper, against a lush tropical backdrop. A friend went
with us on the trip, so I'm not sure who held the camera. Dylan
looked at the picture a long while, asking all sorts of questions,
all but the one I feared most: *Mama, but why did you leave?* How
can I tell him that the trip was one of the saddest times of my
life, that we came home early because his father and I were so
unhappy? How can I explain that even in paradise you can be so
lonely and cold that you feel like you could drown in the very air
you breathe?

OTHER NIGHTS, AFTER leaving Dylan, I have two, three glasses
of wine, one after the other, when I get home. After one very
bad time, I drink a bottle and call my brother in Hawaii, whom I
haven't talked to in months.

I cry on the phone, and he listens with quiet patience. As my
words slur out, how embarrassed I am, how sorry. Our father died
of cirrhosis ten years ago after a lifetime of hard drinking. That
drinking defined much of our childhoods, and beyond. Our existence echoed with the clink of cans and bottles, was shadowed by
the hazy half-light of bars. At fifty-nine, his body finally surrendered. And my brother and his wife took care of our father in the
last stages, so how can I call my brother, drunk and weeping, and
ask for solace, absolution?

I try to tell him what is killing me: not just leaving my son these nights, but knowing that it is just beginning. That I will miss so much of his life, and that it will never, ever end. The price of leaving is this unbelievable pain. And worst of all: the terrible, terrible truth that given the choice, I would do it again.

THAT PHONE CALL showed me the way it could go: a walk down that long, slow hill of alcoholism. At the bottom, it is dark and cold, but also blissfully numb, and what is left of me would live there. I know the path. It courses through the blood of my family. I've seen others go there, many others. Those who do aren't always able to shed that darkness. Most don't come back at all, like my father. A long time ago I tried to figure out what led him to drink. What fear, what regret, what crimes did he try to wash away? Was part of it guilt over his children—over his choices that affected my brother and me?

This is my challenge now: to veer from that path. To be my own light, and if there is a higher power out there, to seek it too. I'm not alone after all; decisions made now are shared with my son. I didn't leave my marriage so that he could have half a mother.

For now, though, there's a bottle of wine in the cabinet, next to a box of pancake mix. I bought it yesterday, a cheap merlot that's not too bad. You see, I still have a glass now and then, when Dylan is at his father's. It is uneasy company on moonless nights.

CHAPTER 8

The Art of Jerry-Rigging

Sparrows use many materials to make a nest; observers have found nests made of mud, paper, candy wrappers, cigarette filters, cellophane, Kleenex, thread, twine, and feathers of other birds, among other things.

—JOHN K. TERRES, *THE AUDUBON SOCIETY ENCYCLOPEDIA OF NORTH AMERICAN BIRDS*

MARCH, THE LAST month of winter, and dinner's on fire again.

The oven's thermostat is broken, so it heats up to about six hundred degrees in no time. Cupcakes are a challenge, but I manage more or less. It's all in the timing.

This has gone on for a month.

In the meantime, my landlord searches for a new part for the oven, an appliance that must be as old as I am.

I can't seem to make it work.

I thought life would be smoother by now, that I'd be settling in, if not into my awful new routine, then at least into my new surroundings. But the forest house has issues that patience and my pen can't fix.

The Runaway Oven is the most dangerous of them, with Most Annoying Award going to Running Toilet. Last week I got so fed up with it that I tied yarn around the handle thing so I could turn off the water. In the Annoying category, Honorable Mention is surely Broken Curtain Cords, which droop like grimy necklaces across the glass door. I usually pin these up with hair clips, but after a while, the clips slip and slide on the fabric.

The Yuck Award would have to be Leaky Well, which makes my bathwater the color of Earl Grey tea. My hair is turning a garish burnt sienna.

The list goes longer, but those are the top four. At least for this week. Most of the problems around here are too petty, or too embarrassing, to call on the landlords' help. They're such nice people; I hate to bother them. So, fully embodying the divorced woman cliché, I jerry-rig. It derives from *jury-rig*, from the nautical term *jury mast*. This refers to a temporary mast raised when a ship's normal mast has been lost due to storm, or battle.

It seems appropriate that it originated with a ship on the ocean— no wonder things go wrong. It reminds me of driving with my grandmother to pick blueberries in Oregon. On our drives we'd see old houses and shacks, furred with moss, slung with tangled blackberry vines, rotting inexorably into the soggy earth. Like foundering ships.

My grandmother would shake her head and say something like, "I'd like to take a hammer and nails to that place."

And she could have fixed them up. She could do just about anything with her hands. Many of these talents she taught me when I was in my teens and early twenties: knitting, sewing, macramé, making pasta and bread from scratch, gardening, watercolors, even stained glass. At one point she fashioned her own darkroom out of a large closet, where she developed her eerily beautiful black-and-white photographs.

Over the years this precious knowledge has slipped away from me, atrophied from disuse like vestigial skills of the domestic female. I wish she were here. She could whip this place into shape. But, really, why can't I? What's with this jerry-rigging? Maybe these habits are hardwired from childhood. As a single mom watching every penny, my mother had to call on a thrifty resourcefulness that knew no bounds. In one place we lived, she slapped up magazine photographs on the ugly bare walls and painted them with varnish. *Voila*: makeshift wallpaper.

A handle falls off, and you use pliers to turn on the faucet from then on. No pot holder? A T-shirt will do. And so on, until your whole life is lived like this, and you and your mom find yourselves bedding down in the back of your pickup truck in the Safeway parking lot because there's not enough money for a motel room.

Where does this line begin, when compromise turns to sacrifice? For me, it's when I don't believe I deserve any better, when I accept crumbs—from relationships and jobs to the clothes on my

back. The habit eventually colors your life, making it easier to al-
low coldness and criticism, then small cruelties. Over time your life
is propped up rather than standing on its own.

I know a woman who, when a lightbulb goes out, doesn't
bother to replace it, and instead relies on the other lamps.
Gradually, room by room, the whole house has become dim; being
in her house is an existence in perpetual dusk.

If it weren't for my son, I probably wouldn't change much. But
he should have better.

And though I'm tired and scared of the future, spring is coming, a time of renewal. I can feel it in the forest, a gathering of
energy beneath the cold.

At Ace Hardware there's a tool kit on sale. I'm going to get
it, and also stock up on supplies—nails, screws, hooks, extension cords. I'll pick up some boxes of lightbulbs because we—I—
deserve to live with light.

CHAPTER 9

Damaged Goods

It is interesting that the common house mouse, so much despised as a pest, occasionally gives voice to a birdlike trilling song. This has been described by observers from many parts of the world. However, the song is very rarely heard.

—OLAUS MURIE, *A FIELD GUIDE TO ANIMAL TRACKS*

I N MY MIDTWENTIES, I lived in the sexy harbor town of Lahaina, on the island of Maui. I was working my first job out of college as an account executive at a public relations firm. Our clients were tourism-based, and our biggest fish the Maui Marriott. One of my main duties—hard to believe now—involved schmoozing at the Marriott's oceanfront Makai Bar. I had an expense account to abuse, and was given great assignments like whipping up a piña colada for Herbie Hancock in his hotel room.

Maui at that time was a blissful concoction of sophistication and rural, small-town life. You could peruse expensive art galleries in plastic flip-flops and then go watch your neighbor's kid as Mary Poppins in the school play. I wore colorful rayon sundresses and flowers in my hair, and I hung out with friends who had jobs like cocktailing and selling suntan lotion on the beach. One night I'd be served a five-star meal at the Four Seasons, and the next morning I'd eat a fish taco from a lunch wagon with sand between my toes. Almost every evening, at beachside bars, we'd watch the setting of the sun, a giant mango melting into the nearby sea.

I pretended to be an adult in this sultry playground.

I was also dating the bass player of the aptly named The Penetrators, a band of swarthy hunks who played volleyball by day and rock 'n' roll by night. They woke at noon and crashed at three or four in the morning. Kenny and I had lots of heady fun but didn't last—it was rum-soaked, tropical wildness.

One night, at a family gathering in Wailea, my brother made a comment I will never forget. The circumstances are hazy now, but there was the usual backdrop of tiki torches and rustling palms, and our father was with us. I was twenty-five and newly single, and someone suggested my brother find me a date for some event or other.

My brother replied, "I wouldn't wish my worst enemy on my sister."

This caused a lot of good-natured laughter, mine included. I was absurdly proud of my reputation as a reckless romantic, which had begun my first year in college at the University of Hawaii. During my undergraduate career I dated an athlete, a valet, an

MBA student, a very rich playboy who'd never had a job, and one or two others who've receded from memory. It didn't help that my father had always made fun of my "conquests," as he called them. He wasn't mean; if anything he was rueful, and I suppose my escapades reminded him of his own younger days, and his regrets.

But sometimes I wish he'd given me a little more direction in matters of love. And yet, what could he have said that would have settled me down? Over the years the memory of my brother's words—of that moment—has become less humorous for me, and more sad, like a slowly fading photograph of a party scene no one remembers.

My own heart now lies in my chest like a crumpled pillow. There's only enough room left for my son. In fact, romance flicks serve as my version of horror movies. I watch them on the edge of my seat, peering through my fingers as the heroine decides whether to knock on the heartthrob's door and proclaim her love. *Don't do it!* I warn. *Run!*

Still, the earth keeps turning. For the first time in years I'm noticing men notice me. It makes me want to hide. But where? That landscape has changed forever.

I know a woman who hasn't been kissed in twenty years. She says she can't tell which is scarier—never kissing again or not wanting to.

The other day a man, an artist who's always paid me a fair bit of attention, asked if he could paint me. *That's a new one*, I thought, and declined politely. I went away feeling the old flattery, but also dismayed. He's a good painter—I've seen his portraits. What of me could he possibly want to capture?

CHAPTER 10

Birdsong

Songbirds, such as the hermit warbler, sing from favorite perches in trees, either within or close to cover, where they are reasonably protected from attacks by hawks or other predators.

—JOHN K. TERRES, *THE AUDUBON SOCIETY ENCYCLOPEDIA OF NORTH AMERICAN BIRDS*

I HAD TWO DAYS' notice. My mother was coming to stay with me, indefinitely. Sky, my mother's pastor, called with the news.

"Your place makes the most sense. Besides, you're her daughter," she said. "We're putting her on the next plane."

I said okay and good-bye and felt the anxiety stir, then sit up and flap its wings. This anxiety had always lived in my gut, making a nest when I was a small child and never leaving. It has been ever-watchful for the past several years.

My mother bought a one-way ticket from New Mexico, where she'd been living in a trailer with her husband for the past five years on land that bordered the Gila National Forest. She was breathless much of the time, using oxygen at night. Doctors prescribed Ambien and Xanax, which she hated to take, and thyroid medication. She couldn't sleep or keep the weight on. Worst of all, her ears "pounded" at night, which, coupled with severe sleep deprivation, brought her almost to the point of collapse.

Despite rounds of CAT scans, EEGs, MRIs, and a blur of visits with medical specialists, no one could figure out what was wrong. The stress of it all was affecting her marriage. For so many reasons she had to get away—and then there was the fact of the elevation of their land: nearly seven thousand feet. She simply couldn't get enough oxygen.

I knew all of this; I just didn't know how bad it had gotten.

THERE'S NO ONE ELSE. The burden of that phrase—and the shame of calling it a burden—weighed heavily for the next forty-eight hours. I looked around my cozy house, this sanctuary carved out of the chaos of divorce. I looked at my small couch with its neatly placed pillows, then imagined her overflowing bags (in the best of times, my mother can be described as "messy").

I already shared a bedroom with Dylan; this place had no room for another adult. How would I write—one of the few sane things I'd been able to hold onto, besides my son? More unsettling—the knowledge that I could barely take care of myself. Naturally, things were still horribly tense with my husband. Each day was a minefield. How could I offer anything of value to this foreign version of my mother? Where had the real mother gone—always bright and dynamic, tall and take-charge beautiful—whom everyone loved for her sheer life force, her endless can-do energy? Who was this stranger described by the pastor: frail, scared, and too exhausted to even talk on the phone?

The stories I'd heard, the ones I'd envisioned as scenes in a movie, suddenly became real. Her endless sleepless nights, the daylight hours spent just one step ahead of the tears. How finally she'd taken off running into the New Mexico countryside and was later taken to the hospital for observation. Suddenly I pictured not an actress, but my mother, running across the desert rocks, running, running.

THEN SHE WAS here on a cool evening on the first of May, thinner than I'd ever seen her, with her deep-set eyes shadowed and bloodshot. All she wanted at first was a hot bath—the New Mexico trailer only had a cramped, dribbly shower—and a cup of herbal tea. For an hour she soaked while I set about making her bed on the couch and arranging her things. Although she had only two bags and an armful of books, she'd rented an oxygen machine from a local medical supplies store. It was the size of a small refrigerator, and ten times as loud.

That first night, as the motor vibrated and rumbled like a small car, I slept about two hours. I lay in bed, terrified by the loss of silence—I hadn't known until then how deeply it soothed me, hadn't understood how quiet can *quiet* one's thoughts.

We compromised the next night, using extension cords and tucking the machine in the garage. Unfortunately it turned out she needed the noise to drown out the pounding in her head, but not wanting to disturb me, she suffered until morning. When I woke up she was desperate and distraught, reminding me of the mother who emerged at times during my childhood.

"I'll hitchhike east," she said, her hands trembling at her sides. "I'll take some money and just start walking east."

"No you won't, Mom," I said. "Get yourself together; this isn't helping. We'll figure it out. We'll bring the machine in. I'll get used to it. It's okay. It's okay."

I could see that she believed me. My mother has a dramatic side—in fact, she always seems most alive in a crisis—but this was different. It was clear that she needed the oxygen, and the noise, much more than I needed quiet. And in that peculiar way that helping someone else can minimize your own problems, my life suddenly seemed manageable again, the way through each day less hazardous, and my steps more sure-footed.

SHE STAYED FOR three months, the first one with me, then alternating the following weeks between me and her friend, who had a lovely extra bedroom and bathroom. Mostly she slept those first few weeks, a long figure heaped in blankets on the couch. She took long, hot baths twice a day, and walked with me in the forest. It was Dylan, though, who seemed to bring her back to life. In the mornings, as I watched from the kitchen, he'd pull back the blanket that covered even her head, as if unwrapping a present, and lightly touch the hands held to her face.

"*Grandmaaa*," he'd sing softly, like a little bird. "*Grandmaaa.*"

How did he know to be so gentle? Gradually she'd open one eye, then the other, to be greeted by Dylan's grin. What woman can resist her grandchild's smile? In this way she was eased into those first mornings. We'd have coffee and breakfast and brace ourselves for the day.

SHE GOT BETTER. I took her to doctors in Reno and baked hearty breads and muffins. She read Westerns and rested. My brother Dace and his wife made her dinner and watched movies with her and made her laugh. Her friends took her to AA meetings and lunch. But she always wanted to come back to the forest house.

IT WASN'T UNTIL June, though, that I noticed her old self coming back. She hauled out a hose and began watering the dry grass around the porch, for one thing, and she spent a lot of time on the porch looking out at the trees on the Diamonds. One day she called me out and, with hands on her hips, announced it was time to plant.

"Herbs! Wildflowers! Pumpkins!" She turned in a slow circle as she surveyed the new grass, clearly imagining so much more. "Can you see it?"

This was good news. While my mother and I have a lot in common—love of books, art, nature—she leaves me in the dust with the garden. She always threw herself into planting, loving it so much she never even wore gardening gloves. My childhood was surrounded by her blossoms and sprouts and brimming pots. My grandmother was like this too; her backyard on the Oregon Coast was taken up by rows and rows of snow peas, carrots, lettuce, bright yellow and orange marigolds.

Later that day, Mom showed up with a trunk full of pots and soil and seeds and seedlings. For the next two weeks she and Dylan, who was right beside her all the time, spent a good part of the afternoon digging and planting and watering. He loved pointing out the different "oarbs" to me, and I loved sitting on the porch near them, grading my papers, and smelling the new scents among the pine and juniper.

I read somewhere that trees welcome your suffering. That their roots run deep and they have no limits for your pain, that all you have to do is share it with them and they will take it and the pain will ease. And so, if my mother could begin to heal here, couldn't I?

CHAPTER 11

The Blue Jay Show

To us, the song of a bird is a source of delight; to the birds, singing is essentially a social activity—though perhaps not lacking pleasure for them as well.

—NATIONAL GEOGRAPHIC SOCIETY, *THE MARVELS OF ANIMAL BEHAVIOR*

WE DON'T HAVE TV. I can't stand the noise, the commercials, the static it creates in my thoughts. When I was married, every other month or so I'd go to Reno to get some heavy shopping done, and I'd stay overnight in a motel. This was my escape, and though I have no love for the city of Reno, I relished these getaways. After a long day of driving and dodging shoppers, I never could resist flopping on the perfectly made motel bed and watching some TV, remote in hand. It never failed, though, that after an hour or so of switching channels, I'd feel as if a hole had opened up in my head and my brain was slowing seeping out.

AT THE FOREST house, we make do with a laptop and Netflix now and then. The real entertainment, though, lies just outside our door. With three large picture windows and a sliding glass door, it's as if we have the Nature Channel on 24-7.

The best show, by far, is the Blue Jay Show. In the early spring, there was just a pair of Steller's jays, but by May, I counted six individual birds. Just the sight of them—feisty and plump—makes the cats tremble. Steller's jays, as opposed to scrub jays, have jaunty crests atop their heads, like plumes on a helmet. They're by far the most boisterous bird (or beast) around here. They're bold, like seagulls, and brash, like crows, but they seem to have more personality. Mark Twain quoted a miner who lived alone "in a lonely corner of California, among the woods and mountains . . ." who said: "There's more to a blue jay than any other creature. He has got more moods, and more different kinds of feelings, than other creatures; and, mind you, whatever a blue jay feels, he can put into language."

I'd have to agree. After reading up on jays, I learn that they have an astounding "vocal array," consisting of the following categories: song, call, scold, zeep, zraanh, shlenk, rattle, chuk, nhyuk, wheeze, distress screech, snarl, kuk, beg, poit, half-poit, and wah. Some of these sounds are accompanied by "wing fluttering" and "bobbing movements," and all have complex communication functions—such as hashing out territorial disputes, or for use as an "intrapair contact note."

As far as I can tell, they spend a good part of their day yelling at the cats, who disrupt their meals: *Be gone! Off with you!* This combination of loud vocals and snappy appearance is why they remind me of tiny pissed-off Roman soldiers.

Around four, just before I start dinner, they hop from the ponderosa pines to the black oak, not twenty feet from the porch, screeching out commands. *Bring food! Pancakes! Crackers! Now!*

These birds are omnivores, and they eat just about anything, with most of their diet consisting of vegetable matter (acorns, seeds, fruit, and other plants) and animals (insects and small vertebrates like snakes and field mice; they'll eat carrion too). So I give Dylan whatever's on hand—bread crusts and stale oatmeal cookies or old cheese, maybe—which he scatters on the grassy place beyond the porch.

Then Dylan and I sit at the kitchen table, turn our chairs to face the window, and settle in to watch the show, which is by turns suspenseful and hilarious.

It begins with the birds. The jays hop to lower branches, twisting their heads from side to side, eyeing the snacks and the general terrain. They "rattle" and "kuk" among themselves, strategizing for a while. Finally one swoops down, landing with a flourish on the grass, where he makes a stand. The others watch intently from their nearby perches. By now, one by one, our three cats have slunk out to the porch. Cleo lies in wait under one of the Adirondack chairs; Rosie and Max stretch out on the edge of the porch, like black loaves of bread, with only the slightest flicker of their tails to reveal they haven't turned to stone.

Cleo always charges first, though she's the slowest of the cats. She never has a chance. She retreats, ears down, eyes to the ground, her dignity smashed as she reclaims her spot under the chair. This emboldens the jays. Then Max and Rosie each give it a try, and though they're more stealthy than Cleo, they've never bagged a jay either. But it doesn't stop them, every afternoon, from trying.

With such neighbors, we're never bored, we're never really alone. This realization surprised me, until I read something in Gene Logsdon's wonderful *Living at Nature's Pace*, about his youth on a small rural farm, surrounded by hundreds of acres of wild country. It was in the '40s and '50s, so imagine this scene without technology. Yet even then, he described an "innocence," and wrote that living there "brought a tranquility to our lives, turned our focus inward." Humans have always felt the periodic urge to retreat.

I grew up like him, some of the time. In the '70s we lived in liberal Mill Valley, California, and my mother taught us to love nature. We had the basics—television, phone, car—but we went camping all the time, and she hauled us off on hikes every chance she got. She seemed to me always distracted at an elemental level, as if she were searching for something always out of reach. Now I wonder, was it herself she was seeking?

Then one day, when I was seven or eight, she went nuts and attacked the television. She staggered out to the back porch with the hulking RCA in her arms and hurled the thing a good five feet onto the concrete, where it landed with a spectacular crash. Or maybe she took the heavy end of a chair to it. All I really remember is the rage, and the sound of a crash, and her triumphant silence.

When she killed that TV, she was only thirty-one—and in the throes of a second divorce while raising my new baby brother and me. Living here at the forest house, I'm beginning to understand her more. Maybe she needed not just simplicity, but clarity, too—as a woman, a mother, a person, and she knew instinctively that one way to achieve it was to turn off the noise and connect to the natural world.

It's been a more peaceful process for me. I'm reminded constantly of how my life is just part of things. And it struck me then, how very real this forest is, how it's not a show, not even *like* a show, but life itself, on its own terms. In *The Outermost House*, Henry Beston's account of a solitary year on a Cape Cod beach, he described the birds there as "not brethren, they are not underlings; they are other nations, caught with ourselves in the net of life and time, fellow prisoners of the splendour and travail of the earth."

Dylan is learning this early, that we are just a part of this place we share with other beings, and so too the wider world around us. That the jays' dinner is just as important to them as ours is to us. It seems these are good lessons to learn, and learn again.

It reminds me of that line from e.e. cummings, "(now the ears of my ears awake and / now the eyes of my eyes are opened)."

Living here is recreating innocence for me, even at times a kind of purity. Dylan, of course, is like all children already innocent; he's captivated by the smallest happenings—the meandering path of a sugar ant, the daily demands of a blue jay, the chagrin of a once-again-defeated cat. And so am I.

CHAPTER 12

Outsiders

Muskrats, only weighing two pounds, lose heat easily and their solution is to become more tolerant of their fellow muskrats. Even nonkin muskrats gather in a lodge and huddle together for warmth.

—Ronald C. Bazin and Robert A. MacArthur,
"Thermal Benefits of Huddling in the Muskrat"

S ometimes it is hard to live in this town. This county is a rugged, starkly beautiful place—made up of arid ranchland and sweeping desert pasture, with the sharp scent of sage and bitterbrush drifting over the land. For years I'd been coming here to stay with my mother, who lived on twenty-three acres of wild rye and rabbit brush. I found the whole place almost exotic, resonant with the fading Old West, and I loved the slow, quiet pace of life.

Eight years ago, when I was between jobs, residences, and men, and still grieving my father's death, this seemed the best place to rest, and restore myself. Though I planned to stay only a few months before moving to a friend's cabin to write a book on the Oregon Coast, I soon met the man I would marry, and this has been my home ever since.

Lassen County's economy, once teeming with mills and mines, is now anchored by three prisons. PBS even made a documentary in 2007 about Susanville, which was partly based on an essay I wrote in 1999: The film, *Prison Town, USA*, was skewed in a few ways, and understandably despised by the townspeople. Though I wasn't part of the filmmaking, I've never lived it down.

Whether you favor the prison industry or not, in a small town, it makes for a mostly conservative, predominantly blue-collar population. In many ways this county has more in common with places in the Midwest or Wyoming, and definitely with our neighbor, Nevada, whose border is less than a day's walk.

I've never fit in.

I am not only still a "newcomer," but also a tree-hugging writer, possessing suspicious graduate degrees and a liberal sensibility. I've long since found the artistic people, gravitating to these dedicated folks like a bee to pollen, and attend as many of the "cultural" events as possible. There's a terrific symphony, for one, and the arts council is more active all the time, showcasing the talented artists, writers, and musicians of the area. The college I work for hosts a popular music series in the summer. We even have a farmers' market where a vendor sells local, organic produce.

But for the most part, activities revolve around church on Sundays, the county fair, hunting, holiday parades, and Tea Party gatherings. During the 2008 election, Obama's few supporters kept quiet: A colleague put a magnetic Obama/Biden '08 sticker on her car that she would remove when parked. She feared someone might take a key to the paint.

The only other person who's seemed more out of place is B.J., the hairdresser at Headquarters Salon. He's done my hair since I first got here; we know each other's secrets. Years ago he gave me permission to write an essay about him called "The Only Gay Man in Susanville, California" (which I never wrote). Is it any wonder he ended up at the forest house when he found himself without a place to live?

HE MOVED IN to the empty upstairs, where he'll live for the summer. Our entrances are separate, and despite our plans to get together and chat, whole weeks go by without us actually seeing each other. To a solitary type this is a relief, but also sort of too bad, because he's not only fun, but quite remarkable to look at. Well over six feet, 195 pounds of muscle, fabulous surfer-blond hair, and the clothes! Dolce & Gabbana, Giorgio Armani. He zips around in a shiny Eclipse coupe, although I'm not sure how he physically fits into it. In this place of macho-man pickup trucks, it's quite a car. You can hear it coming from a long way off, the engine's throaty rumble, then view the sleek red vehicle zooming through the trees.

As neighbors, albeit reserved, B.J. and I are courteous and kind. In his first week he lowered down a Tupperware of home-made pasta sauce in a bag with a rope, from his porch down to mine. I leave pastries picked up at the farmers' market on his door-step. He's also astonishingly predictable: up at six thirty for coffee, off to the gym at eight, back at ten fifteen for a shower, then to work at eleven, home at nine—five days a week. On Sundays and Mondays, his days off, he usually goes to visit friends in Reno.

"It's time to get out of town!" he'll shout as he zips down the road.

I feel a flash of envy, because sometimes even the sanctuary of the forest house is not enough. When Dylan was with his father, I spent the night away in Quincy, and another time in Truckee. Both towns are artsy and quaint (they have half a dozen daily yoga classes, and the restaurants offer locally grown food). I stayed in humble motels and drank wheatgrass shots in funky coffee-houses that reminded me of grad school. I roamed the aisles of lavish health food stores and marveled at the long-haired men and jasmine-scented women.

Best of all, not a soul knew me.

See, they seemed to say, as they glanced at me and then away, *Life goes on. Come visit whenever you like. In the meantime, you'll be okay.* And the next morning, refreshed, I would drive back to my life.

THE FIRST FEW nights, when B.J. came home, I was startled by the sound of footsteps above. He's a big guy, so each step is clearly audible, but it didn't take long before I got used to the noises: *step-step-creak-creak. Step, pause. Step-creak.* After a couple of weeks, his evening arrival became a part of things.

Why are you here, in this town? I want to ask him. He makes me think of my professor friend's pronouncement, that our town has three kinds of people: the drifters, the stickers, and the stuck. I, at least it seems, am in the last category.

B. J. moves out in September, wanting to avoid the winter, and who can blame him with his schedule and that sports car. The forest house is a place to dig into in the cold season, stocking up on food and wood and books.

I can't predict what this winter will bring—the last was so hard. One thing I do know: At times I'll miss the rhythm of a neighbor's footsteps in the evenings, and knowing that if I should ever need someone, I don't have far to go.

CHAPTER 13

Jimmy B

California's last known naturally occurring wild wolf is trapped and killed in Lassen County in 1924.

—DEFENDERS OF WILDLIFE

O NE FRIDAY NIGHT in mid-June, deep into a book on the porch, I get a distressing call from Bonnie at the Humane Society. She tells me about an alley cat who lives in a part of town that, for cats, is a war zone. He'd been shot in the eye and was hiding under a building.

I was pretty sure I knew the cat, a year-old male who was shy but friendly after being fed now and then by some kindhearted folks. About six weeks ago, we'd trapped him, and I took him to the vet to be neutered and vaccinated under our feral cat grant. Transporting ferals is something I do about once a week, so I had only a vague memory of a dark gray tabby with large golden eyes, crouched in the wire trap that we drape with a towel as a token of comfort.

Some of the cats let out sorrowful moans all the thirty miles to the vet, but that tabby was quiet. It was as if, having lived in a filthy, junk-filled alley, roamed by dogs and hoodlums, he knew the futility of protesting fate. He lived, like the AA folks who left cheap kibble on a dinner plate for him out back of the Fellowship Hall, one day at a time.

On the phone Bonnie tells me she'd spent hours luring the terrified cat into a carrier, and then set him up in her laundry room with food, water, and a painkiller wrapped in salmon. In the morning she'd take him to the vet to have his eye removed, with the Humane Society's emergency funds. I know the score. Bonnie already fostered too many cats. She'd let him recuperate there a while, and give him his meds, but he had to find a home.

WHILE HE CONVALESCES in a kennel at Bonnie's, I write my column for the paper and title it "Lassen Humane Society Seeks Donations for Jimmy B." (We named him Jim Beam, Jimmy B for short, because he'd been fed most of his life by alcoholics.) They print the picture I took of him, a close-up of his face and the one eye crisscrossed with ugly sutures. The caption: *Jimmy B recovers from a gunshot wound.* His expression is wary. It's a heartbreaker. When I look at that photo, I see the best and worst of humanity.

In less than a week, we have almost $1,500 in donations at our post office box, mostly in $5, $10, and $20 amounts, with *for Jimmy B* written on the checks. This floors us. Susanville is a hunting town, a ranching town, and animal welfare doesn't register much. Besides, these are tough economic times. But Jimmy B has struck a chord.

Still I know it will be hard finding him a home. Most people seem to want attractive pets—I know this from talks with Judy at the county animal shelter. Too old, too homely. Colors matter—tabbies and black pets are too ordinary. The workers are usually forced to euthanize the less cute ones because of lack of space; somewhere between twenty to fifty cats a month in our small county are "put down." It's not surprising we sometimes call the shelter "death row."

I realize one morning that I've already decided. Dylan thinks it's a great idea—he'd have a whole zoo if he could.

WHY DOES EVERYTHING come at once? That very afternoon I discover two orange and white kittens behind Dylan's dad's house (my old house). They're about six weeks old, abandoned in a broken carrier in the alley with a urine-soaked blanket. It's a chilly, wet day, and will be a cold night. I scoop them up, thinking frantically of anyone who might foster them until we can find a home. Bonnie says no way. Finally I call the shelter, but since they're at overcapacity, the kittens come home with us.

We call them the "Creamsicle cats." Their eyes are infected, and they sneeze constantly. In the morning they wake with eyes matted shut, and their poo is dribbly, but at least they use the litter box. My other cats despise them, hissing, glaring, growling.

Meanwhile, while I hunt down antibiotics for the kittens, Jimmy B waits in a kennel at Bonnie's. I keep thinking, *I already have three cats. I've committed to one more. What am I doing with two kittens?* It reminds me of a line from Mark Doty's memoir about his dogs, a musing he has after adopting a golden retriever during a tragic and overwhelming time in his life: "There's a certain dimension of experience at which the addition of any other potential stress simply doesn't matter anymore. Oh, say the already crazed, why not?"

Sure enough, the kittens take over. They bounce around the room, catapult off the couch, hike with tiny but sharp claws up my calves. At night they try to nurse my neck, purring like tiny Volkswagens. Dylan loves them, and they're adorable, but I'm determined to find them a home, knowing that Jimmy B, fragile as he is, has to wait until I do.

I TAKE PICTURES of the kittens and post flyers, and within two days, find a home for them with a single mother of three who's just lost her beloved dog. That day Bonnie bundles up Jimmy B in a "transition kennel"—an enormous cage—and brings him up to the forest house.

"Keep him inside your house two weeks," Bonnie warns. She's been rescuing cats for a long time, so I listen carefully.

Jimmy B has his own ideas. Although he seems happy, rolling onto his back to be scratched and eating heartily, he wants out of his "transition kennel," and then he wants outdoors. His fur, when petted, comes out in clumps—a sign of stress. This is a cat who's never been in a building, let alone a cage, and he's been kenneled for three weeks. Shelter workers call it "kennel stress." I let him have the run of the house for three days. He meows, breaks several slats on the window blinds, and even claws down the rubber seal alongside the sliding glass door. He stares outside, nose to the glass.

So on the third day, when it dawns with bright sunshine, and the other cats are lounging on the porch, yawning blissfully, I relent and open the door.

"Okay, Jimmy B, here you go."

Shrinking himself to the size and posture of a weasel, he slinks around the corner of the house. The phone rings, and when I come back out, he's gone. Over the next hour Max, Cleo, and Rosie come back, but Jimmy B, the alley cat who's never seen a tree before, has vanished into the forest.

I call Carla, my cat-rescuer neighbor. "I let him out. He's gone."

"Uh-oh," she says. I tell her about the broken slats, the meows, the seal on the door. "He'll come back by evening I bet," she offers in a hopeful tone. "He'll be hungry."

THAT NIGHT I stand outside for a long time. From the forest house at night, I can just see the amber glow of the two state prisons through the trees, even though they're nearly twenty miles from here. It's said you can see Susanville's prisons from Sacramento, two hundred miles away.

The prisons sit out on the desert basin, the land spreading out in all directions, and I always wonder what it must be like to see that expanse when you are fenced inside and can, at best, simply look out at it.

An unhappy marriage can seem like that. Barbara Kingsolver wrote that a bad marriage is like "a slow asphyxiation." And when you have a child, the bonds feel even tighter; how then can you break free of what is slowly killing you? The physical, the emotional cages we're in or put ourselves in—are they really so different?

"You bet," the inmate would reply.

I know because as their teacher, I read their essays. Their freedom, they write of it like the lost love of their life. Sometimes I have to take a break, not because I'm tired of reading, but because I have no more room for their pain.

Jimmy B doesn't come back that night. I walk the forest again and again, calling for him. I put out little piles of tuna in a large circle around the house. He still isn't back Sunday morning, when Bonnie calls to tell me the thrilling news that the Sheriff's Department has collected the entire cost of the surgery, $365, over and above the $1,500 that we've used to establish a "Jimmy B Emergency Fund." She wants to do a follow-up photo of the cat right away and run a thank-you column in the newspaper.

"It'll be great for the Humane Society's image," she says. "We need a feel-good story for once. Take a picture of him all cozy on the couch or something."

"Right," I say, getting off quickly before she can ask how the famous cat is doing, and go look for Jimmy B again.

All that day, there's no sign of him, even though Dylan and I walked and called for him many times, until it grew dark. I wonder how our voices sounded, plaintive and light above the forest.

Over the years, for various reasons, I've had many pets go missing. Jimmy B's disappearance wore on me like no other. It wasn't merely that I'd been entrusted with the care of what had become a minor local celebrity, or that he'd rejected my pleasant home, my offerings of love, food, and quiet comfort. It was that, despite my good intentions, I'd made the wrong call. I *knew* he should have stayed indoors another few days, but I let him out anyway. My bad judgment made me uneasy, and off balance, and doubtful about my fitness as a caretaker for anyone or anything. The hours ticked by like small punishments.

AT TEN AT night, full of dread, I finally call Bonnie.

"Listen, I have some really bad news," I say. "Jimmy B's gone. He's been gone since yesterday morning."

Silence.

"I should have kept him in longer, so he'd know me and this place better."

"Yes, you should have."

In the tense pause that follows, I look out the glass door and see a strange shadow streak by in the moonlight, some small animal. I know the shape of my cats in the dark. Cleo's bouncy trot, the sleek lope of Max and Rosie, their black ghostly figures.

"Wait!" I say. I turn on the light, and there is Jimmy B on the edge of the porch, one eye wide as he crouches. "Bonnie, I see him—you won't believe this—but I see him right now!"

He'd come back. I went outside and fed him two cans of wet food. He let me pick him up then, and I brought him inside. He slept that night under my bed, ventured out in the morning for breakfast and a belly rub, then slept the rest of the day. At dusk, he wanted out, so I let him go. He's not my prisoner. This time he was gone for two and a half days. Lately he's been coming around morning and night, every day. He no longer slinks away when he leaves. He walks slow and straight into the trees.

CHAPTER 14

The Sleeping Place

Although preferring to den in hollow trees, [the raccoon] frequently is found in caves, mines, woodchuck burrows, drain tiles, rock ledges, and even in barns and under buildings. Curled up in a ball or stretched out flat on its back with forepaws over its eyes, the [raccoon] sleeps the day away.

—LEONARD LEE RUE III, *PICTORIAL GUIDE TO THE MAMMALS OF NORTH AMERICA*

WHEN DYLAN IS gone, I often wake in the night with the startling awareness that I'm alone in the forest, far from anyone. I've had insomnia for years, so this is familiar—these hours are more like a destination I go to than a time I live through. Near the end of my marriage this place felt like a steel cage. Now that I live in the forest house, it's opened up into a yawning, featureless expanse.

In this landscape I wander, searching for peace, for somewhere to rest my worries, for somewhere to bury my guilt at having left. The wandering, if it goes too long, turns to quiet panic. To calm myself I imagine the trees outside, their womblike formation around the house, and this helps a bit. I try to sleep again, at first on my own with meditation and prayer, then finally with herbs or, if it's very bad, an antihistamine. With these aids I descend into sleep soon enough. There will be a price to pay in the morning of course: My body will feel weighed down with wool blankets; my head will be overrun with clouds.

Hours later, after coffee and activity, I'll come back to myself. Sleep is better when my son is with me.

This is the difference: I hear breathing.

We share the bedroom; he is just on the other side of the bookcase. The blankets rustle when he shifts. He sighs. We are together here—alive, warm, safe. Everything else sits on a shelf. Now and then, I wake briefly to get up and adjust his covers, to feel his warmth beneath them, to rest within his deep, deep peacefulness.

CHAPTER 15

Prison Town Prayers

Among many larger herbivores, social organization modifies the nature of home ranges. [A deer] cannot disappear in a hole in the ground but rather depends on running to escape . . .

—EVERETT WILLIAMS JAMESON AND HANS J. PEETERS,
MAMMALS OF CALIFORNIA

EVERY SMALL TOWN needs a bookstore like Margie's Book Nook. I'm sure the owner, David, remembers the depressing arc of books I bought over the years, the plot unfolding every few months in the form of each new title I slid onto the counter. First the books on how to manage as new parents (unforgettable line: "Having a baby is like a bomb going off in your marriage"). Then how to keep your love alive, with fun exercises that are, in actual practice, sad and ridiculous.

Next in line came the "last chance" book(s), whose save-your-marriage exercises were no longer fun, but arduous and desperate.

About a year later I crept up to the counter with a thick volume about how to divorce without losing your mind, body, bank account, and/or soul; close on its heels, I purchased one that promised to teach me how to coparent in this grave new land. The last book was not for me but for Dylan, which described, from a cheerful child's perspective, the adventure of having two houses: "This is my backyard fort at Mama's."

I always blushed, as if I were buying something unseemly, like questionable ointment from a pharmacist, or some terrible erotic thriller at the video store. But David never commented on these books, and I knew he wouldn't gossip. Like a good bartender, a bookstore owner knows how to be discreet, and, when necessary, how to distract a customer near tears.

Such havens are rare in a small town, where there's almost no place to hide. You can't go anywhere without running into half a dozen or more acquaintances. It's impossible to drive down the street without passing a handful of drivers you know. At the county fair in July, at least a hundred people will nod or wave, or come up and chat. Folks are aware of, and care about, others' lives. This intimacy can be wonderful, especially during hard times; there's always some spaghetti feed going on to help out someone in need.

But when you're on the wrong end of rumors, which run through town like tumbleweeds, living in a small town can be oppressive.

My great-grandmother Emma knew about rumors. She grew up in Sunne, a tiny Swedish village, with an inn, courthouse, sheriff's residence, parsonage, and market. I looked it up on a map. If you imagine Sweden as a finger dipping into the North Sea, with Norway to the west and Finland to the east, the province of Värmland would be just above the fingernail, and Sunne a tiny freckle within.

This was a lovely place in the early twentieth century, layered with lakes and rivers and rolling plains bordered by forest-clad hills that used to teem with bears and wolves and other wild animals. There Emma, who bore six children in under ten years, went about her life as mother and wife of Olaus, with whom she owned the butcher shop and market. Theirs was a turbulent marriage, and Olaus, a hard-drinking man, left often on cattle-buying trips.

In so many ways it was a stifling life for a woman. One day Emma saw an advertisement for the theater and opera, and against social convention, she went alone. In the dark she would focus on one actress, her aliveness, and make it her own, and take it home with her, where it must have helped her be the housewife she was supposed to be. In a time when it was considered a frivolous luxury, she went to the hairdresser. Sometimes she wore fancy hats, or went on walks alone. She held dinner parties when Olaus was gone. Everything she did was noted and talked about.

When things were very hard, did Emma imagine she was on a stage, and that these daunting years were only a scene in a very long play, with a beginning and an end and eventually a time to rest? I wonder if Emma sometimes became lost between the world of the stage and the world of her home.

I WAS ALSO the wife of a business owner, and known. Many times over the years, someone would approach me and start chatting, asking about my husband or the store, and I'd have no idea who he or she was. I've never liked the feeling of being *noticed*.

This feeling spiraled when I moved to the forest house. As time went on, I didn't know who knew, or who didn't, and I scanned people's faces for signs of judgment or curiosity. I found myself dressing nicer than I used to—no sweatpants! Sunglasses provided another layer of protection. And Dylan, I made sure, looked tidy. Outwardly, I revealed no sign that anything was less than great.

I wasn't crazy though. Enough incidents occurred to fuel this paranoia; once, at Susanville Supermarket, one of the pastors' wives looked at me from several carts away with such despair I thought she might break down right there in the checkout line. "I'm praying for you," she said. Heads swiveled in my direction.

She's a kind woman, and she meant well, but it didn't help my confidence to know that I was such a disaster that people were compelled to pray for me. In the beginning, my sister-in-law put our family (in coded language) on the church prayer chain. I imagined a hundred or so pleas lifting above Main Street, drifting toward heaven like pale butterflies. Eventually this stopped; did they accept defeat, that we were a lost cause? The prayer list is long and ever-changing—a lot of tragedy goes down in a prison town, and maybe there just wasn't enough room for us anymore.

Some days I feel my eight-mile drive home is a flight from town, like I'm an escaped convict going to a hideaway. Nothing less than a long walk in the trees can calm me down.

IN A SMALL, conservative community, church is ever-present. It pervades a town's consciousness the way the smell of a lake might suffuse a resort town. It can't be easily ignored, as is possible in cities, or dipped into partway, such as in liberal small towns, with their Unitarian kumbaya gatherings. There's a sense that all the good people go to church. I used to go, and sometimes miss it— that feeling-good feeling, the approving glances, the sense of a net of pulsing humanity around me, all of us in rows like an army of rightness. It never felt natural to me, though, probably because I was raised to suspect anything remotely religious. Also, going to church required closing off parts of my brain.

The first time I went—this was before we were married and we were casting about for meaning—I left feeling shell-shocked.

First of all, there was singing. A lot of singing. This was called "Worship." It went on so long I started looking around, wondering if this was the wrong place, that we'd wandered into some kind of choir practice, and feeling very nervous because if this was church, then what would the sermon be like? And how long would it last? No one else looked confused or impatient. They were animated and bright, dressed in cheery colored clothes; the men scrubbed, the women purposeful. I'd never been more uncomfortable in my life, as my past and present sins slithered around my ankles.

We switched churches and kept going, week after week. And some months later, for a while we even worked in ministry, in a recovery-based program. We went every Friday night, and this was where I felt at home, with the addicts and gamblers, the bingers and the bombed-out. My parents were alcoholics after all; this was familiar territory.

One night I stood up in front of a room full of people and gave my testimony as a Codependent. People cheered when I was done! There was a band—most of them former drunks and meth users and all saved by God—and they were fantastic. Each week we stood and clapped and were regularly brought to tears by the healing all around. We sang, "I'm trading my sickness, for the Joy of the LORD!"

Then the head pastor, a man I revered and who had married us, had an ugly affair, wiping away my communion-wafer-thin trust; at the same time, infertility descended upon my body and soul like a slow, dark plague, and it stayed there for years.

THE OTHER DAY I reread some of Anne Lamott's essays, in which she writes with wonderful reverence—and irreverence—of her born-again Christian faith. As California-native, Bohemian-type writers, we have a lot in common. We once appeared together when my first book came out; I was her warm-up act at the event, which for her was the equivalent of a jam session, but for me, Madison Square Garden! Since then I pull out her writing when I need a laugh and a kick in my self-pitying ass.

In one of these essays she writes about a close friend whose toddler has terminal cystic fibrosis. During this tragic time, Anne describes feeling like a kid being spun around in a pin-the-tail-on-the-donkey game and being "so lost and overwhelmed and stressed that I couldn't even remember where the wall with the donkey was—or even in what direction it might be found."

Finally, she remembered that for her, the wall with the donkey on it was Jesus. I envy her clarity, her sense of faithful direction. These days, the wall for me is the forest, in whose peaceful quiet I can offer up my own prayers to whoever is listening.

I may go back to church one day. They would welcome me with genuine warmth, and no questions asked. But I need to be alone for a while, maybe a long while, and who but trees and animals have the patience for that?

CHAPTER 16

Trip Wires

Today's American black bears are genetically predisposed to retreat and flee rather than to fight when threatened.

—Matthias Breiter, *Bears: A Year in the Life*

M Y AUNT KATHY, who lives across the state in vineyard country, came to stay with us for a few days in July. She's a nature-lover extraordinaire, so besides getting to see me and Dylan, it's a real treat for her to visit the forest. One afternoon she went walking down our road with him and my seven-year-old niece, Sheila. They took a bag for leaves and rocks, and I went out to the porch to straighten the woodpile. Their voices lilted through the trees.

At one point the tone of their voices changed, and it wasn't until they returned that I learned the reason why.

They'd discovered a few trees embedded with old barbed wire. Kathy told me I should get some wire cutters and free the trees, which had been in bondage like this for decades. The kids nodded beside her, and Sheila described the sap that had leaked below the wire "like hard tears." They were clearly outraged at the sight of the poor trees.

The land around the forest house is littered with these stretches of rusty wire, the useless remnants of old fence lines. You'll walk along and then suddenly realize that just ahead, like an enormous sinister spiderweb, lurks a tangle of barbed wire. Some of it's buried in the ground, with twisted offshoots suspended eerily in the air. On snowy days, I came across wire emerging from smooth expanses of snow, stark as black sutures upon the white surface.

Wherever the wire is, it's half-hidden and usually stuck fast in a tree or underground. For a long while my walks—at least the ones off the road—gave me the feeling of navigating a minefield. Even before Kathy's nature walk, for months I'd been worried about Dylan, about my niece, about children who might come up to play here when summer came. I worried about the animals, too—my own and the wild ones around here, especially the deer that run, startled from the sound of my car coming up the drive.

If I let my mind drift on these walks, the irony would creep over me, that this place in which I feel so free was once restrained, fenced, the way I'd sometimes felt in my marriage, and at times living in this isolated town, and beyond I'd think of the razor wire enclosing the prisons. Even though the wire here is useless and scattered, it's still dangerous, even deadly.

Over the next few weeks, every time we walked by a certain juniper, with the wire cutting into its belly, Dylan would point and tell me to "get that bobbed wire out!" It reminded me of how children must be taught compassion, how it's not instinctive in humans—like motor skills or language—and that a child who cares about the lives of trees, and animals, and bodies of water, will be that much more able to care for the lives of people. Not just certain people, but all kinds of people. So often compassion is meted out, like emotional coins, to this group or that, to this species or that. But for me, compassion is a continuum across the spectrum of life.

ONE AFTERNOON WE finally get busy. I borrow some welding gloves and fence cutters and, while Dylan collects kindling nearby, bend to work on the wire. It's tough and slow going, much of the wire hopelessly intertwined. Barbed wire is nothing like rope or hose or even steel cable. You can't simply "roll it up" because it's not inert; it has a life of its own.

I drag bundle after bundle up the hill to the driveway, some lengths fifteen feet long, snagging all the way on bushes and fallen logs.

In the end, there's a truckload full of it, waiting for my neighbor to haul it to the recycling plant.

Getting rid of that wire took two afternoons, and my hands ached for days. But it was done, finally, and it felt wonderful to sweep away the debris and take care of this land. Life is sometimes like this too, isn't it? We sense threats at the periphery of our world, the subtle and not so, that keep us corralled until we clear them away.

Anyway, now the forest feels more inviting, and it makes me think of how much our family loves trees. Maybe it's our Swedish ancestry, the ancient memories of dark forests lingering in our subconscious. My grandmother taught me to care for trees when I was very young; on the way to her home on the Oregon coast we would drive through the womblike tunnel of trees that is Van Duzer Corridor. This corridor, which burrows through thirty miles of the Cascade Mountain Range, is thick with coils of ivy that choke the trees within; more than once she'd pull over, grab her hatchet, and lunge into the forest.

It was a futile chore, hacking at the tenacious loops of ivy, but she was compelled to free at least some of those trees. I've always loved this about her, about all the women in my family, who'd rather jump in than look away.

CHAPTER 17

Coming To

In hibernating ground squirrels, it is difficult to detect any heart-beat. It is difficult to tell if the animal . . . is dead or alive.

—BERND HEINRICH, WINTER WORLD

NOW IT'S TRULY summer. The creek below the forest house is almost gone. I used to hear the path of the water all the way from the porch, the insistent murmur, the mournful tuba notes of the toads: sounds that seep into the ground. In the spring, Dylan and I spent many afternoons there, exploring, gathering rocks for his rock garden, kneeling on the sandy bank to touch the silky green reeds that swayed in its currents. Now the bed is dry, and only a few spots are damp, shaded by willows.

We were glad to see the bridge we built of sticks is still there. Thank goodness it's a seasonal creek, fed by the mountain snows and rain, and will return in the fall. Until then, we have more and more sunlight, ever so gradually each day, so that the world is like a giant eye opening after a long sleep.

I too have felt an awakening, a falling away of whatever kept me safe from my emotions. Now I cry fully and laugh loudly—often at the smallest things—overthrown by feelings I used to try to keep at bay. I'm not as afraid of them anymore. These emotions pick me up and carry me like waves before passing through.

And one startling day, I wake to warmth. Dylan's with his dad, so only the cats share this miracle with me. I step onto the porch in a loose nightgown and feel the breeze, so reminiscent of swimming, the way water flows over the skin, or fingertips trace the curves and hollows of a body.

I'm not sure why the sensation feels so astonishing; I've been in all kinds of winds a thousand times before, and surely the air must have eddied around my throat and arms, must have skipped down my spine like this. Maybe it's the gentle, even tentative, nature of this wind.

And maybe it's being reminded of what it's like to be touched. How did I miss this, and where have I been?

Very suddenly I'm awake to myself.

CHAPTER 18

Neighbors, and Other Distractions

Trace a brook to its source and very likely you will come eventually to
a spring . . . A thread of water flows unendingly across the lip of the
pool, but makes barely a sound as it trickles down the gentle slope.
Only when the stream has joined forces with others and has begun to
tumble across steeper slopes will its whisper become a full-fledged song.

—ROBERT USINGER, THE LIFE OF RIVERS AND STREAMS

A DONKEY LIVES ABOUT half a mile down Diamond Fall
Road, behind the big gray house that borders Palmer Ranch.
I've never seen this creature, but judging by the stentorian sound
of his braying, which comes at random times, he could be the size
of a small pickup truck.

This donkey, whom I call Big Jake, was the last thing on my
mind when I woke an hour before dawn, feeling just rested enough
that returning to sleep would require an angel's small act of mercy.
I surrendered at four forty-five and went out to the dark morning,

where I settled into one of the deck chairs with a book light and Sara Maitland's meditative *A Book of Silence*. In it she explores the nature of silence, and our relationship to it. It seemed an intriguing way to start my writing day, and so, rather satisfied with myself, I began to read.

The temperature outside was softly cool, the way it is in late July before the sun rises. The moon was still high enough that I had to lean my head back to see it straight on, and the stars shone like miniature beacons. Embraced by solitude, the moment was solemn, sacred. Maitland's book reflects on the power of religion to break silence, and I read her musings on the presumption that an awful void existed before God brought language, and therefore life.

On the porch, at first quiet and dark, it soon became clear that I was in a place wholly alive, with the low thrum of crickets, and the questioning purr of a cat around my ankles, and the almost palpable sense of *forest* surrounding me. The idea of a void was hard to imagine—but peace, that was much easier.

And as I contemplated the metaphor of *breaking* silence (why not *opening*? Or *entering*?)—just then—the donkey stepped up to the world and trumpeted out a stream of honking sounds so thunderously, so forcefully and absurdly clamorous, that they must have carried the length and breadth of the forest and beyond; doubtless they could be heard from the top of Diamond Mountain.

I laughed out loud and closed the book.

How many times do I have to be reminded I'm not alone?

CHAPTER 19

Tree Scars

A mature tree is capable of producing thousands of seeds, but not all of these seeds will germinate, and not all of those that germinate will grow into mature trees.

— THE ILLUSTRATED BOOK OF TREES

W E'RE LOOKING FOR tree scars in the Diamond Mountains. The snow at the top has finally melted, allowing access to the logging roads that wind up its steep slopes. A biologist with the U.S. Forest Service has come along as my guide.

For months I've looked out on these mountains, so close I can walk to them in minutes. They fill the view from my house the way air fills a room—quietly and completely. When, in the middle of winter, I moved to the forest house, it was this all-encompassing view that somehow led me to believe that I just might make it.

In four hours we never see another human being. Searching through stands of white fir and Jeffrey pine, we are looking for signs of injury—a mark, a cut, an indentation of some kind. Often it's fire; other times a tree's been cut with a saw, or gouged by machinery or a vehicle, and I think of the barbed wire scars of the trees at the forest house, their "hard tears" of old sap.

We first come to a Jeffrey pine with a vertical slit twenty feet high and a few inches across. It looks as if a sharp object has slashed the tree in a long, straight line. At the base of the pine, Tom shows me how the tree is growing around the injury with layers of bark, protecting itself, like a coat clutched tight to a body.

Some of the scars are more obvious than others: the slashed trunk of the white fir we pass, the result of a logging skid ramming the trunk, probably fifteen years before during a harvest. Low on another Jeffrey, we see a triangular scar the size of a footstool, its interior charred from a decades-old fire. For any wound, the tree must overcompensate, pulling energy from branches and leaves to nurture the site of the injury.

IN THOSE FIRST months at the forest house, when my son was at his dad's, and the nights were long and dark and the silence stole under my skin, I gathered strength from the trees—western juniper and Jeffrey and ponderosa pine, mountain mahogany and willow down by the creek. Their peaceful endurance inspired me. On my walks I'd often stop to rest my face against a strong trunk, and breathe.

In between snowstorms, when the snow sloughed off the trees, I began to notice that some of the trees looked damaged—bent at odd, painful-looking angles, or the trunk had split, or branches had gone missing. I kept thinking of those broken trees—what happens to them, how do they survive?

THE METAPHORS OF tree scars, how quickly they descend as we walk through the quiet forest. I think about the many varieties of survival: not just physical, but emotional; not just for a person, but for a family. And the word *injury* itself—the first connotation is a wound (a cut, gash, abrasion); the second is an offense (abuse, affront, injustice); and the last is harm (damage, affliction, suffering). What is the nature of my family's injury?

For the tree, the wound makes it more vulnerable to insects and disease, to drought and other fires. So too our family was, and still is, more vulnerable to loss and separation. Like the tree, how were we forced to compensate for our injury over the decades? How far off course did our destiny veer? The injury, it seems, began with the marriage of my great-grandparents, Olaus and Emma. Forced to marry, they had no love at the start. Six children and a decade later, all that remained was bitterness. Then one November night, while the children watched from the upstairs landing, Olaus and Emma's father began a fight that nearly killed Emma's father: my great-great-grandfather.

Olaus, to avoid prison, fled to America. Emma followed soon after; five of the children would, one by one, over the years, also move to America to start over. This leaving, this loss, continued in their children and their children's children. In some ways, I believe we are all still recovering from events a century ago, in a small village in Sweden.

LATER, I'LL READ of the principle of uniformity in nature, an idea first raised in the late eighteenth century. It's basic to any study of the past. When applied to the study of trees, or dendrochronology, it means that one can look at climate, slope, soil, and make assumptions about the past. In other words, similar conditions present today must have been present in the past. For trees at least, it can also be said that "the past is the key to the future." That is, by knowing past environmental conditions, scientists can better predict, and manage, such conditions in the future.

In some way, this applies to people, doesn't it? This will actually be my second divorce. This time there's a child. He's as innocent as I was when my parents separated, so long ago. From then on, I saw my father just a handful of days a year. Longing planted itself deep within me, giving birth to seeds already inside; it was this longing that never went away, irrevocably complicating every relationship I've ever had.

FINALLY WE FIND what we really came to see: a cut stump of a centuries-old tree, where we can find the hidden scars. It's wide enough for two to sit comfortably. There in the cross section is the long-ago scar enclosed by bark and obscured from view. Counting the rings, we decide the injury must have occurred 150 years ago, when the tree was maybe twenty years old.

I learn then about tree rings, and how it's not a simple matter of counting them to find a tree's age. It is true that most trees add a layer of wood to the trunk and branches, next to the bark. This happens in the spring, when moisture is plentiful, and the tree devotes its energy to producing new growth cells. These first new cells are large, but as summer presses on they shrink until, in the fall, growth stops and cells die. This year-by-year record or ring pattern tells us much. For example, if the tree lived through a drought year, that ring will be narrow. When moisture is plentiful, the ring will be wide.

Yet sometimes, if too many changes occur in a year, more than one ring will appear. In a year with extreme midsummer droughts, for example, several rings can form. And some years have no rings at all. This is rare, and most rare in oak and elm trees. In fact, the only recorded instance of a missing ring in oak trees occurred in the year 1816, also known, sadly as it seems to me, as the Year Without a Summer.

We examine the stump more closely. The tree rings curve toward and around the site of the damage, reminding me of river water flowing around a stone. And I stand astonished at this evidence of the secret—and sadly beautiful—life of an injury, of a long-ago event of untold violence that, though concealed, is very real when exposed. Visible or not, the scar does not fade; the tree does not forget.

WHEN MY GRANDMOTHER died, five years ago, I couldn't grieve, and even now I can't enter the particular sadness that holds a place inside me. Not yet. What if I could lay myself bare the way you can expose the life span of a tree? What if I could read my soul the way you might a ring pattern? *Here,* you could say, and with a finger touch the start of the scar, *here I am two years old, when my parents ended their marriage.* Then drawing your finger further still, you could say, *These years here are good years and full of love, but then see right here—this is where my father died, and my life narrowed. Here, right here, is when my grandmother died.*

Looking at the whole of a life, and the pattern of its rings and scars, you might then be able to say, *This is how my soul managed the loss. This is part of the reason I made the choices I have made.*

And what of the life I am living now? Ending a marriage, a family. Losing so much precious time with my son. How deep will these wounds reach, and how will I compensate for the damage? How will they be presented on the portrait of my life, and more importantly—of my son's? Will he, one day in the future, be able to make sense of them, and will he be able to find forgiveness in his heart?

TO EXPOSE THE life of a tree scar, you have to cut it in half: You have to sever the tree from itself. You can also cut a wedge from a living tree to discover its history. But to do so is to risk killing the tree.

Examining the life of a soul is not the same. To reveal truth, to discover its source and span, however painful, we don't have to die: On the contrary, we become able to live more freely.

CHAPTER 20

Fire Season

The Western Fence Lizard thrives in the mountainous forests of northern California. It avoids danger through constant vigilance and fast reflexes.

—Robert C. Stebbins, *A Field Guide to Western Reptiles and Amphibians*

TWO YEARS AGO, a wildfire almost destroyed this house and the forest around it. From a satellite map, the fire appears as a long, oval shape, brownish in color and surrounded by the green of trees. My house, on the map, sets impossibly close to the fire's perimeter: According to the map's scale, the distance is 330 meters, or just over a fifth of a mile.

The Cheney Creek Fire, as it was eventually called, burned 2,300 acres.

I remember the fire. I lived in town at the time, with my husband and toddler, and stood transfixed in the front yard, watching as smoke curtained the western sky, and how the fire's glow swallowed the sun at the horizon. It was as if the sun were bleeding into the land. I listened to the low throb of helicopters hauling canvas barrels of water, and I remember the feeling that something violent, and uncontrollable, had come to find us.

In the past decade, several devastating wildfires have burned nearby. When compared with the latter half of the twentieth century, this is startling; there were only two fires in those fifty years, from around 1950 to 2000. Experts blame this lack of fire on the suppression policy of the last hundred years, providing fuel buildup that would eventually, when ignited, create calamitous wildfires. Before that, in the 1860s, settlers brought livestock whose grazing kept fuels to a minimum; earlier still, Maidu Indians started fires to encourage acorns, berries, roots, fibers, and to flush game and collect grasshoppers.

For each previous century, the records fade; only a few fires can be documented from the 1500s.

It could happen again, here, this summer. I try not to imagine these trees outside my door—the western juniper where the Steller's jays scold my cats, the black oak, the ponderosa pine—all of them consumed in columns of flame, the air black and oily and the creek water boiled and vanished. I've come to love this land that I've walked in snow and sun, know its every path and curve, the game trails and the circle of matted grass where the doe lies with her two fawns in the late afternoons.

And I love the wild look out my door, the knee-high grass swiveling in the wind, love to watch Dylan and the cats stalking through it—but when the landlord came to mow it down in the interest of fire suppression, it was all right with me.

FIRST THING THIS morning, before it gets too hot, I walk up the hill behind the house. It's so steep I have to lean forward into the climb and watch my steps to avoid sliding down the loose soil and rock.

Then, thankfully, I reach a flat plateau, an acre square or so, tufted with bitterbrush and juniper, and here I find a flat rock and take a rest. Further on, the hill resumes and rises to a ridge that frames half the sky. Behind me, across the valley, the Diamond Mountains fill the view—only to the east is there a break in the horizon. It's as if I sit below the rim of a giant cup, whose small spout pours into town, eight miles away.

I'm afraid to continue on ahead, and it's not only because of mountain lions.

Just beyond is what's left of the Cheney Creek Fire: hundreds of acres of burned land and thousands of dead trees. Thin, gray, leafless, held upright by skeletal roots, they have the look of solitary shipmasts anchored in an empty seabed. Some have succumbed to last winter's storms, scattered like thrown sticks on the ground.

For months I've taken walks in every other direction, the way one might take a longer route to avoid a cemetery. At first I was

worried about the fear it would provoke in me, of seeing the de-
struction and how near it came, of having one more thing on my
list of worries—a wildfire. How swiftly it would rush down the
mountain over these dry slopes and envelop our house.

Then, as I grew to love the trees outside our house, my fear
expanded. I didn't want to walk among the dead trees, the scalded
land. It can take twenty years at least for a forest to even begin to
recover from a fire. Didn't I have enough to grieve? I didn't want
to link my damage with the land's.

And yet—here and there young pines have sprouted, tiny
spots of green, so incongruous on this barren beige landscape, like
youthful freckles on a ruined face.

Sitting quietly at the edge of the burn, I'm not alone. A finch in
the mountain mahogany, the song of another bird and the answer-
ing call of yet another, small butterflies, a scuttling lizard, a trio of
red ants at my feet. How strange to come so close to the fire's path,
to sit on the edge of its violent aftermath. How good it is to see
that even the worst thing passes, and in time a new peace is made
possible.

CHAPTER 21

Dianna's Table

In the more gregarious, group-living species—the ungulates, many rodents, and in particular the primates—the mother only begins the learning process. Every individual that the growing animal comes into contact with can contribute something to its education.

—NATIONAL GEOGRAPHIC SOCIETY, *THE MARVELS OF ANIMAL BEHAVIOR*

EVERY DAY THAT Dylan isn't here, I write. And once a month or so, for the past eight years, I've gone to Dianna Henning's writing group. Actually it's called the Thompson Peak Writers' Group, which makes it sound more formal than it is. Dianna, who writes gorgeous poetry, is a fairy-tale godmother sort, with a mellifluous voice and brown hair the texture of dandelion fluff. She wears flowing clothes; she's like a walking waterfall.

Sometimes the world throws you lifelines, and Dianna's group was one of those for me. Without it, I sometimes think, I might have stopped writing years ago, which for me is a soul-killing thought.

The meetings take place in the nearby tiny town of Janesville, in the living room of her lovely home in the pine-strewn hills. It's the sort of house in the sort of setting that one might expect to arrive via horse-drawn sleigh. Usually three to seven people show up; some are new at writing, some—like Dianna and Jordan Clary—have published widely. Mostly there's a lot of warm encouragement, but I always come away with some terrific feedback that makes my piece better.

I also just have a good time in her warm house that smells of oranges and cloves. She serves treats like goat cheese and almonds, fruit tarts and half a dozen kinds of tea. Each meeting begins with announcements of writing contests or readings—usually too far away, in Reno or Sacramento, maybe, and in this way I'm reminded of another world out there, one I used to live in, where people talk about art and books and poems so poignant they leave you speechless.

A COUPLE OF years ago, I tried to give up writing. My work hadn't brought in money for a long time, and it seemed unfair to persist at something that wasn't contributing to the household. Besides, being deeply unhappy at the time, I felt I had little of worth to put on the page. By then, a four-hundred-page novel was gathering dust in a closet, and three or four other book projects had made it to the fifty-page mark before sputtering out like cheap candles.

I tried pitching smaller pieces to magazines, but kept hitting dead ends and brick walls. It may be easier to have a chat with Barack in the Oval Office than to land a query on an editor's desk at O, *The Oprah Magazine.*

Meanwhile my first book continued to drift toward the outer reaches of the universe, further and further from human contact or memory, like a defunct satellite. Sometimes I'd remind myself of those mildly glamorous moments—being flown to Minneapolis by Random House and picked up by a media escort for a Midwest book tour. Or appearing with *Fight Club* author Chuck Palahniuk in front of five hundred people. Or hearing myself interviewed on NPR's *Fresh Air.*

I held onto these memories, stored much like the newspaper clippings and posters and photos that took up space in my file cabinet. Once in a while I'd rub salt into the wound by checking my book's sales rank on Amazon.com. This practice, called "ego-surfing," is never a good idea (unless you're Elizabeth Gilbert). The day after my *Fresh Air* interview was broadcast, my rank was number 277, as in 277th out of about 2,500,000 books. After just checking now, in 2010, my rank is currently number 365,831. I also learned that there are fourteen used copies of the paperback available for the price of $.01 each. Yes, that's one penny.

Presently in my garage, eighteen cases of my first book (twenty-four copies per case) lie in neat stacks on shelves along the wall. They remind me of the cartoon on my refrigerator—two guys are in a forest, one wearing a business suit, the other in rumpled writer attire. They're standing at the base of an enormous tree made of stacked books. The business guy says, "We used your unsold copies to build a tree, but it's not the same."

With my unsold copies, we could probably make a very nice fort for my son.

It didn't make sense—something I loved to do, and possessed some talent for—why should it be nearly impossible to make a living at it? I felt a little like an injured athlete who paces the sidelines at the games. Was I injured? Or was I just one of those players who has one decent season, showing lots of potential, but then goes on to disappoint so many times she's benched for life?

Yet I kept going to Dianna's. I couldn't stop writing. I looked forward to those mornings at her table. Thinking about it, jotting down notes, observations, ideas. I read books on craft, took my journal with me on walks where I'd find a spot and write a paragraph that had been haunting me all day.

There are things that rescue us, that pull us back from the edge. For my mother it's gardening, holding the earth in her hands and making something come from it. For my aunt Kathy, it might be the ocean. For me it's books—writing and reading, the give-and-take of words. These things connect us to something larger than ourselves.

My mother has a bumper sticker on her jeep; it says, ART
SAVES LIVES.

CHAPTER 22

On Wood and Warmth

*Early nesting requires constant brooding of the eggs during cold or
stormy weather; sometimes the nest and even the incubating bird are
covered with snow, but the devoted mother generally succeeds in keeping the eggs and the center of the nest dry and warm.*

—ARTHUR CLEVELAND BENT, *LIFE HISTORIES OF NORTH
AMERICAN BIRDS OF PREY*

FALL DRIFTS IN on a heat wave. It hasn't rained in so long that
dust sails behind us as we drive up our dirt road, then settles
over the junipers in a grimy beige mist. Yet the nights are growing
cool, sometimes dipping into the thirties. There's been no morning
frost, but above the house, the oak leaves have turned every shade
of red at the branches' ends, like tiny brilliant sunsets.

Earlier in the summer, when prices were their lowest, I bought
two cords of wood from a man named Russ. He'd advertised by
parking his beat-up trailer, stacked with neat rows of wood, in the

Grocery Outlet parking lot. WOOD 4 SALE was scrawled in red paint on the side. For $140 a cord, he said on the phone, he would deliver a load of split ponderosa, lodgepole, and juniper to the forest house.

A few days later, on a sweltering July afternoon, he crawled down from the cab of his old pickup, looking like a stick of wood himself, with gnarled arms and crags in his cheeks. He wore a pirate-style red scarf round his head and was missing several teeth; he could have been thirty-five or fifty-five. Because I live in a prison town, I couldn't help thinking: *Meth*. And then: *He knows where I live.*

But he was polite and swift with his business, cigarette in mouth while hurling wood piece by piece with gloved accuracy onto the flat earth beside my porch. After he got his money, he trundled back down the road with a wave. Still, it was the first time I thought seriously about getting a dog.

FOR WEEKS, WELL into August, the pile of wood lay there in the summer heat, tall as a man and twice as wide. Lizards and spiders made nests in its cool depths, and Dylan had great fun poking a stick around the edges. Often one of the cats would perch on a log up top and preen. There was no need to write "stack wood" on my to-do list—the spectacular chore-in-waiting greeted me several times a day as I came and went. It even seemed to grow slightly higher over time.

THOUGH IT TOOK a while, I finally realized this procrastinating was about not wanting summer to end, and that as long as the pile sat there in the sun, the rain wouldn't fall, the cold wouldn't come, and I could continue to hover within the warm, bright summer like a bird circling a cloud that veils the ground far below. I wouldn't have to face the reality I'd filed away: that judgments would soon be filed with the court, the six-month "divorce process" would be complete, and I would be utterly on my own, with no going back.

This blissful holding pattern was a dangerous place to stay in much longer. I needed to shop for health insurance, to close some accounts and open others, to begin looking for more teaching work, to stop avoiding the truth when people asked "How are you doing?" And I needed to stack the two cords of wood outside my door.

Fortunately the landlord had a wheelbarrow, and with Dylan bringing sticks and lengths of peeled bark, and I ferrying loads through the heavy dirt (a bit like steering a listing ship through churning water), we stacked a row of split logs that ran the length of the porch. The wood came just below the windows so as not to block our view of the forest. This took a few days, sweating in the afternoon heat, and as the rows took shape so did my satisfaction.

Despite the sweat, this was of course easier than procuring the wood in the first place. It was Russ the woodcutter who had driven into the forest, gone to work with chainsaw and ax, loaded the wood into a truck, and then thrown each log to the ground at our house. Still, our rows of wood felt like a great accomplishment, and I enjoyed the work immensely. Dylan also seemed quite proud of himself.

In *Winter*, Rick Bass writes of the forty or fifty cords of wood (there were so many I lost count) he gathered to survive a Montana winter in a lone cabin, all of which he cut and split and hauled and stacked himself. Half the book seems devoted to the getting of wood, and his love of it. He liked to watch "the pile growing higher, the fortress, the protection against the cold." Bernd Heinrich wrote in *A Year in the Maine Woods* of the warm glow of satisfaction when viewing his woodpile: "Let it rain, I think; my wood is safely drying. Let the snow and the cold come in the fall and winter; I will *welcome* them."

I've heard others say that wood heat is better than anything electric, and I'd have to agree when recalling how last winter, Dylan would run from his bath to the fireplace to warm himself, how the heat gave his skin a rosy glow, and how he stretched out his hands as if to hold it. The fire's penetrating, almost muscular heat had substance, and along with the dancing of the flames, the play of light in the room, it kept us company in those first dark months.

At one time, the writer Dominique Browning had several fireplaces in her home (even her bedroom), claiming they are the greatest source of comfort (especially, she implies, after her divorce). "When it came time to mend my soul I *needed* to sit in front of a fire."

When Dylan was with his dad, I too spent many nights last winter and spring in front of the fireplace, although it was usually after much work and worry. I was a clumsy and anxious fire-builder—to me it was a necessary, verging on desperate chore that took a ridiculous amount of time and energy. I soon resorted to buying Coleman logs, which only demanded I light their wrapper in a few spots before offering me warmth.

Even so, I didn't have the right rhythm for the longest time, well into April, and usually once a night the fire would start to die, and I'd try to keep it alive. Many nights the house filled with smoke and, nearly sobbing with despair and frustration, I'd be forced to open the windows and door to the twenty-degree air.

Now I look forward to the coming fires—most of the time.

THERE'S NO CLEAN way to heat a house, but at least wood isn't a fossil fuel, and a cycle starts when I spread the ashes into the forest and know they'll be absorbed back into the ground. There is a kerosene heater, with a 240-gallon tank on the side of the house (resembling a very small silo on its side). Per gallon, it's about $3.15, no small change. Wood is the cheapest way for me. Besides, when the power goes out, the heater is useless.

So I look at the fireplace and all it entails with profound gratitude, the way one with a fancy but unreliable car might view an old bicycle. You know when all else fails, you can get where you need to go.

My friends in town use gas and electric heat. Susanna and Jordan have woodstoves as well: efficient, easy to use, and attractive with ornate iron molding. Doors close off the flames, and gates surround the stoves for safety's sake. But I'll keep our fireplace. It's enormous—two feet high and three feet wide—and when it really gets going it takes over the room with its galloping light, and the pistol shot–crack and pop of the fire.

THIS MORNING, WE woke to a cold rain that soaked summer's dust deep into the ground. Tonight, Dylan and I will light the first fire of autumn, and sit side by side as it flickers to life. We'll watch the light brighten the corners of the room and feel the waves of warmth calmly engulf us.

CHAPTER 23

Companions

It is not uncommon to find birds of several species flocking together. One reason may be that such flocking increases the number of eyes and ears available to detect predators . . . Also a mixture of species can take advantage of different abilities . . . it has been shown experimentally that chickadees and titmice are used as sentinels by Downy Woodpeckers . . .

—Paul R. Ehrlich, David S. Dobkin, and Darryl Wheye, "Mixed-Species Flocking"

A MOUNTAIN LION HAS been making appearances. I haven't seen it myself, but others have, a ghostly figure in the headlights. The other day, down on Palmer Ranch, a calf was gutted. My landlord called and told me not to walk at dawn or dusk. He told me to keep my guard up.

I thought about that. What guard would that be? The biggest animal here, my one-eyed gray tabby, Jimmy B, would make a nice mouthful for a mountain lion. And so when the opportunity came along, and even though I didn't want one, I finally got a dog.

Maple was on her way to the pound. A midsized pit-Lab mix the color of pureed pumpkin, she belonged to a troubled family I'd been helping now and then with their pet issues: giving them donated dog food, helping an injured cat get to the vet, transporting Maple to be spayed back in May (paying for half of it while imploring the Humane Society to pay the other half). We lent them carriers and crates. Like many Susanville families, their needs extended far beyond their unfortunate pets, but such small contributions did make a difference for struggling families. At least I told myself so.

Rhonda, Maple's owner, was a twentysomething woman with two sunny-faced boys, a bipolar disorder, and a violent drug-dealing boyfriend perpetually on his way to another stay in jail. Once when I came by, she had a black eye. She told me they'd just been evicted, and she begged me to take Maple, her "baby."

"I just can't handle any more stress," she said with wet eyes— one surrounded by a fading, yellow bruise. "I can't."

We both knew if I didn't take Maple she could end up spending weeks in a cage, and—being a mutt—would likely be euthanized. But there was no room at my house for another animal, especially a dog. Dogs are needy, in my experience, requiring ten times the energy and time of cats. You can't leave them inside for a day or two and take off. I didn't have a fenced yard or a kennel. They need a lot of petting; they follow you around the house. Having four cats and a young child was enough, thank you.

It was Dylan who changed my mind. Now four, he's become a skilled eavesdropper when I'm on the phone. Like a wily junior CIA agent, he'll drop key phrases from prior phone conversations, sometimes hours later:

"Mama, what's 'put down'?"

"Umm, it means go to sleep."

"Why would Maple go to sleep?"

"Do you like Maple?"

"Oh I love Maple so much!"

So in the end I said yes. Rhonda's gratitude made me ashamed, because it seemed a small thing. Still, Rhonda was smiling when we arrived to get Maple (that sweet, gentle animal, who was so wonderful with kids), and the dog came home with us.

SINCE THEN, MAPLE—renamed Mirabella Maple and called Bella for short, has been quietly attached, like a sweater loosely tied around my waist. It's astonished me. Happening upon the right dog has been very instructive for a woman who's never found a very good match in a man. It brings me enormous hope. Of course the comparison works only so long. Bella listens but doesn't talk. She's incapable of bad moods, and graciously suffers mine.

With Dylan, she's an angel, a gentle protector, and when he's here she sleeps at his feet. She's like the dog nanny from *Peter Pan*.

Bella is also lovely to look at. That burnt sienna coat, chest blazed with white, like the colors of a cooking school that specializes in autumn fare. Her head is framed by small, flop-over ears that bounce when she runs. She's the size of all of my cats put together—which is to say, the perfect size for me. She can sit on my lap (mostly), but is happy to rest at my feet, where she reclines with her front paws crossed. This dog, who spent most of her life on a chain without shelter, loves to roam the forest, but never goes too far. I reach for her and she's there. When I do errands in town or grade papers at the office, she snoozes in the backseat of the car. Probably because she was mistreated, she acts like a guest at all times, always on her best behavior.

It took her no time to learn that the cats, no matter how arrogant or odd, were to be tolerated and not chased. Incidentally, it may not be big news to anyone else, but having Bella has taught me that there are two pivotal differences between dogs and cats, which goes a long way toward explaining why the dog is man's best friend. First, dogs have eyebrows. Their ability to alter their expression by moving their brow muscles helps them communicate emotion in a relatively human way.

Cats, who don't have the same mobility, seem to have no expression at all, just a bland, uncaring stare. Life would have been easier for them over the centuries, probably, if they had eyebrows. The only other facial expression that I can see is either extremely pissed off/scared, or sleepy/content. Consequently, it takes a lot of practiced observation to figure out a cat's moods.

You've got to study their body language, particularly the ears and tail. Some men remind me of cats—their faces are fairly unremarkable, you can't really tell what's behind that implacable gaze. We must hunt for other clues. Dylan, like Bella, is a snap to read; hopefully he won't lose that wonderful transparency too soon.

The other difference is what drives cats and dogs. Bella has taught me that unlike a cat, a dog's mission, aside from eating, is to please us. Which is why they obey us. I tell Bella to get into her bed, and she does! I tell my cat to get into his bed, and he blinks. It's not that cats don't enjoy our company, or aren't affectionate. Cats just aren't willing to compromise like dogs. (I want an animal in between—not quite *I'll jump off a cliff for you!* but not *You're on your own, buddy*, either.)

Still, I love my pets and their variety. They make life interesting. And as Bella's playful side emerges I've been saying to myself with a smile, "Bella's got her groove back."

Fortunately she knows when it's time to be fierce. If someone approaches our car in a parking lot, for example, she barks harshly from the backseat, her hackles raising up in a tawny ridge. An intruder—or a mountain lion—would think a bit before taking her on. Now that she's here, I feel better when Dylan's on the porch and I'm in the kitchen.

And when Dylan's at school or with his dad, I have a companion on my walks. It must be a good sign that I welcome this company. Although I may have told others she's for protection, the truth is I've rarely been scared during my walks in the forest. But at times, at times, I have been lonely.

CHAPTER 24

In October

The wind moved in a different way from season to season and
brought the storms in at different angles . . . Even during the worst
of it . . . we were happier than we could have been at home, inside a
house built to keep everything out.

—TOM BROWN, JR., *THE TRACKER*

IN EARLY OCTOBER, my mood sways from melancholy to a
quiet anticipation. Sure, "there's something in the air," but it's
different this year. Because I've always lived in a town or urban
setting, the seasons' changes have always been human-dominated.
For the first time in my life I sense the coming of fall and its changes
in a way I can only describe as "naturally."

I've been used to autumn being announced by my now ex-
neighbor taking a leaf blower to the nut trees in her front yard, and
then raking and bagging the leaves. (I was never sure why she was
in such a hurry to speed things along.) Another neighbor began

preparing for his annual haunted house in mid-October, and so
the sight of skeletons in his elms announced Halloween. Other
obvious signs of autumn: pumpkins and harvest decorations on
the doorsteps. Of course the trees lose their leaves, and the air
cools, but for me the prominent man-made cues drowned out these
gradual changes.

Now, living at the forest house, it's the slow turn of the leaves
of the oak and the sycamore that announce the time of year. Each
morning, sunlight moves another fraction of an inch across the
room, and now flows through the kitchen window. And the sounds
are different. It's quieter. The crickets and toads are gone. The
territorial singing of the birds has faded—only the blue jays' call
remains, and the occasional evening hoot of a great horned owl.

In town, the sounds rarely change. No matter the season, the
cars still start up for prison shift change at five in the morning. The
kids go to school at eight, and the county workers come home at five.

May Sarton, writing from her house by the sea, admits, "I forget how beautiful it all becomes when the leaves are gone. I have a
far wider expanse of ocean, and from my bed can even see waves
breaking on the distant rocks." In his account of a solitary year on
Cape Cod, Henry Beston writes similarly of the change in sound—
that when autumn comes, "There is a new sound on the beach, and
a greater sound. Slowly, and day by day, the surf grows heavier,
and down the long miles of the beach, at the lonely stations, men
hear the coming winter in the roar."

I hear winter too, coming in the quiet.

NATURE IS SHOWING me how to slow down, teaching me another way to ease into another season. I remember the shock of coming home one afternoon to see the neighbor had "cropped" his apple trees—all the branches had been lopped off at the base, leaving a dozen gnarled stubs, like horrid clenched fists raised to the sky. It happened while I bought groceries and took my son to the park. The world outside was always so noisy, it seemed necessary to match my inside world to it. But now the outside is quiet and gradual, and if you want to notice the changes in the world, you have to pay attention.

MY BROTHER DACE, who lives right off Main Street in town, just celebrated his one-year wedding anniversary. His new wife is all I could want for him—and in fact I tried to set them up about six years ago, despite Carolyn and I being very different. She doesn't like silence the way I do. Which is a good thing, because in their house live two adults, three teenagers, a second-grader, four dogs, four cats, assorted fish, and an Arizona king snake. Carolyn also babysits a two-year-old several days a week. At any given time, three televisions will be on simultaneously tuned to different stations.

The house is a thousand square feet.

When my niece, the second-grader, first came to spend the night with Dylan and me, she stopped in midplay and listened, then asked, "Can we turn on the radio?"

"Sure," I said, and put on some music. I forget that quiet takes some getting used to. She brought a DVD movie, but we didn't get around to it. Besides, it wasn't long before the two of them took off outside.

Here they come, running up the hill through the trees. Their laughter sails through the forest like a song.

CHAPTER 25

Survival of the Fittest

A thicket is an impenetrable tangle of shrubs, vines, and small trees. Competition in a thicket is very intense, with each plant trying to overtop the other in an effort to get the most sunlight.

—LEE ALLEN PETERSON, *EDIBLE WILD PLANTS*

MUCH HAS BEEN written about the competitive world of modern motherhood. But can I just say that it's actually real? That even in a small humble town in the middle of nowhere, where having all of your teeth can be a source of pride, we mothers are assessing each other like junior high kids at a Friday night dance?

At least I am.

Fortunately mine is a boy child—I don't think I could take on the added pressure of doing a daughter's hair and dressing her in adorable outfits. It may be sexist, but it's also convenient to say "You know how boys are" when I haven't taken the time to wipe the jelly off Dylan's cheeks, or he's wearing the faded Bob the Builder T-shirt again because the laundry's not done yet.

There's Susanna, the supermom, who sets the standard for motherhood. Her children want for nothing—not love, time, or money. When I was looking for day care for Dylan, she recommended Stephanie.

"I've checked her out," Susanna said.

This endorsement had the chops of an FBI investigation. So Dylan spent his weekday mornings at Stephanie's for a few months until preschool started, and he loved it. Other mom friends constantly impress me. Connie is the mother of two beautiful and wild twin boys who cavort like fawns with loud voices. Somehow, she remains completely unruffled. She also raises chickens, writes a magazine column, cooks gourmet country meals from scratch, and sews her sons' clothes. Crystal—the sexy earth mother—is a brilliant artist with three girls and a boy who could be poster children for an idyllic '70s commune. She blows glass and fixes cars and sings.

All of these mothers create Halloween costumes that could make the cover of *Parenting*. Their diaper bags burst with coolness. They're also younger and married, which means they have to take care of husbands in addition to everything else. Next to them I'm half-assed as a wife, as a homemaker, as a mother. They would disagree and list my accomplishments, but noticeably, none of them are domestic.

Susanna: "But you wrote a book! Oh my God!"

Me: "That was eight years ago."

Susanna: "But still . . ."

Writing a book doesn't make one a better mother, although the reverse might be true. I think it was Anna Quindlen who said that having children, though exhausting, gives one a better self from which to write. (Let's hope so.) The page calls; my son calls. Of course Dylan comes first, but there's always the feeling that I don't give him 100 percent. I'd rather, when he's at preschool, craft paragraphs than design birthday party invites.

I relate to Claire Dederer, who actually paid herself to play with stuffed animals for twenty minutes with her child. "At the end of twenty minutes," she writes in her memoir, *Poser*, "loomed a kind of event horizon of boredom. I would fall off the edge into a black hole."

My mom friends possess something else in common: at least two children. It took me years, and a miracle, to have just one. Those were hard years, living in a town where not having a child is like not having a collarbone. Early on, one of these moms also had infertility trouble, though not as extreme, and only with the first child. She gave me loving encouragement during my years of science fiction baby-making, but usually her child was sitting on her lap at the time, or at least within my line of sight: My friend had been there, yes, and it was wrenching, but not anymore.

Lately, when I watch Dylan playing alone on the porch, against the backdrop of pine and oak and juniper, the old pain circles the edge of my consciousness. If only I could wipe out the memory of that day in the doctor's office, when I learned where I stood on the fertility chart: "Here you are," said the doctor, tapping my age of thirty-seven. It was right where the black line took a steep dive, like a bird shot out of the sky.

The despair is stored somewhere, the years of going to Reno twice a week for injections and ultrasounds, of driving through that barren Nevada moonscape, of watching my medical file grow thick as a textbook. Of trying and failing, each month imagining a tiny hopeful moon rising and falling, cycling through my body only to die again.

Not being able to get pregnant, and having a miscarriage, can carve away your self-worth; the failure settles there like a dark pool in your heart until it runs through you like the blood in your veins. For my mother, my grandmother, my great-grandmother Emma—her first girls coming one, two, three years in a row—children were a given. Twelve children were not uncommon then. Pregnancy and children were a fundamental part of who they were. Sometimes I imagine all of their babies, like those Russian nesting dolls, one nestled within the other, across the generations. What happened to me?

I thought these emotions had faded away. After all, my child is perfect. But grief hangs on, much as lichen clings to rock face. It doesn't get in the way often, but it's there. Maybe, once I had

Dylan, there wasn't room or reason to grieve. But now I can remember, can let those feelings surface, can forgive my body, and myself. There he is, miracle child! It's time to let that old fear, that gripping failure, pass through.

CHAPTER 26

First Snowfall

[The garter snake] must occasionally encounter temperatures low enough to make them sluggish, barely able to move. In such conditions the natricine snakes have shown their great adaptability . . . Caught by an early autumn snow that might immobilize another snake, the garter snake can generate enough heat to keep moving.

— CHARLES E. SHAW AND SHELDON CAMPBELL, *SNAKES OF THE AMERICAN WEST*

I WAKE TO A foot of snow, the first snow this year. In the night it's as if a long swath of white has fallen from Alaska to the tip of California, and we are buried somewhere in between. The tree branches are so laden they are unrecognizable, made to look like the dinosaurs in Dylan's books.

The snow falls thick and fast; thunderous if it were rain, but more than silent in its current form. How can something so all-encompassing make no sound? Even the wind demands to be heard.

After making a fire I go out to shovel the porch and walk-way. It feels good to be doing something so wholly physical—and necessary: If the snow isn't cleared, there will be a slab of ice by tomorrow morning that might not melt for days, or weeks, or even months. People in town predict a bitterly cold winter. I'm reminded of how heavy snow is, the deadweight of it, and as I bend again and again I think of my grandmother's bowed back as she worked in her garden in the long coastal afternoons, in sun and in fog.

Dylan, who would enjoy the new snow, isn't with me, but there will be more, much more. It's only November.

Around four in the afternoon, the scraping of a snowplow—a fabulous sound! It's my neighbor, who lives with his wife and two kids about a quarter mile to the west; we share a part of the road until it Vs between our stretches of the road. He doesn't have to, but he backtracks and plows my section, all two hundred yards, half of it steep and narrow. (I make a mental note to buy him a six-pack of good beer). If he didn't plow, it could be another day or two before my landlord makes it up here.

Now I can get to town. Today's my day to feed. I've got several cats—I never know how many are still alive at any given time—and a miserable chained-up dog I bring food to. The cats, strays turned feral, are at the college. With the administration's blessing, the Humane Society was allowed to set up a plastic bin in the rocks under the juniper tree across from the Correspondence building, where I work. This feeding bin helps keep the cats from overrunning the campus and scrounging in the garbage cans, as they used to do.

Every other day or so, I fill up the bin with donated food. Students and teachers pass by, maybe wondering about the woman crouched in the rocks. Lately I've brought up water too, since the sprinklers are put away until the spring. Whatever they don't drink freezes, and I have to break it up on my next visit. This is a pitiful setup, but it's all I can do. Sometimes I catch a glimpse of these "ghost cats," the gray Tom or the fluffy black with the white star on her chest. I rescued Cleo here, my wonderful tuxedo cat, and because of her, I hold out hope for the others.

Then it's time to visit the dog I call Murphy, who's been isolated and chained up 24-7 (literally) for years. Her "shelter" is an open plastic crate. I've left notes, called Animal Control, even talked to the woman, who wouldn't look me in the eye. I've resigned myself to bringing Murphy biscuits and treats, which I have to sneak in by the back alley. At the sight of me she comes alive.

It's during the winter that the suffering weighs on me most. This weight, the loneliness of trying to take care of these animals— how I longed to share it with my husband. I've always thought, if I had someone to share this with, the relief would be so great.

WHEN I WAS nine, I spent my Saturdays at a card table that I'd set up in front of Cala Foods in Tamalpais Valley, California. It was just down the block from our house on Flamingo Road. There

I'd put out a tin for donations, and a petition and other items sent from the Save the Seals campaign headquarters. I'd sit there all day by myself collecting quarters and signatures, which seems a bit remarkable to me now.

There is something about the *voicelessness* of animals. For me their lack of words makes their presence even more poignant, the way the snow's silence seems to give it more weight. I used to believe that if animals could talk—if a horse or chicken could say, *I'm hungry. I'm cold. This hurts. I want to live*, humans would never be capable of the cruelty and neglect they inflict. But of course even children are often ignored—and what of man's unfathomable cruelty to man? Having a voice to protest guarantees nothing.

No matter, I send a silent thank-you to my neighbor and his plow and keep going, driving in the snow with a trunk full of cat food and a bottle of hot water. A waste of time? Maybe. But if nothing else these small acts will help me sleep tonight.

CHAPTER 27

The Beauty of My Surroundings

As the nests of mammals in general are not as well defined as those of birds, it must be admitted that the best way to identify a nest is to see the maker or the animal itself. This is particularly true of such mammals as shrews, ground squirrels, and mice, which have several species whose habits are much alike, and who build nests following a pattern common to the genus.

—RICHARD HEADSTROM, *A COMPLETE FIELD GUIDE TO NESTS IN THE UNITED STATES*

M Y SECRET CRUSH is *Real Simple* magazine. If it were a man, it would be Kevin Costner about ten years ago: beautiful (but not perfect), friendly, smart, and down-to-earth—and fatally out of my league. He and *Real Simple* only *seem* attainable. Other home magazines are the Clive Owens of the home publishing world. You don't have a prayer of pulling off their soufflés or rose gardens, and you and the editors know it.

But *Real Simple* makes you think that you, too, can easily have a neat and useful medicine cabinet.

For some reason, such goals have forever been out of my reach. My approach to housekeeping is kind of like my cooking—a bit haphazard, a bit on the fly. Most of the time, I tend to tuck, rather than put things away, and a lot of mysterious bundles lurk (sometimes for years) in the backs of drawers and cabinets. I hate recipes and their precision, their mysterious synergy, how it somehow *does* matter whether you use a quarter of a cup of oil versus a third of a cup. In this way I'm like my mother, who cooks by instinct. She's kind of like Jackson Pollock in the kitchen; the difference is that she pulls it off.

Unsurprisingly, I've never earned high marks in the domestic arts.

Yet I love clean windows, a beautiful vase of flowers on a gleaming table, orderly stacks of folded clothes, the invigorating scent of lavender sheets. I adore a homemade simmering soup in the Crock-Pot. I really do long for the *Real Simple* lifestyle.

The forest house is confusing. I've made a comfortable space. Mostly it's clean and tidy. Sometimes it's so lovely I catch my breath. Yet too often light streams in the window in such a way that the dust shimmers along the edge of the windowsill, the wood of the rickety bookcase, the frames of the photographs. Then I notice filmy cobwebs above the curtains and grimace at the thought of the bottom shelf of the refrigerator. I worry that my home will never be "done."

Is a mother's housekeeping influence ever completely shed? Because my parents married several times in their lives (someone once likened the seven marriages between them to cells "uniting and dividing"), I've had more than one influence.

My own mother and my stepmother Kaui, my father's second wife, were my main role models. But they were so opposite, so incredibly different in their views of keeping a house, that I awkwardly settled somewhere in between.

My mother came of age during the dawn of women's lib, when housework symbolized submission. She turned her back on domestic priorities, except those necessary to function, such as having a clear pathway down a hall, or enough room in the sink full of dishes to get to the faucet.

She also lacked a sense of organization except for mostly alike objects—clothes in the bedroom, food in the refrigerator. The finer points, such as gathering canned vegetables on one shelf or organizing dresser drawers, didn't register.

This never bothered me as a child; such upheaval gave me room to explore and make my own messes. Though as I grew older I began to appreciate the serenity of matching silverware at my friends' houses, or the clean expanse of a living room carpet. Nowhere was this more influential than in Kaui's home. She came on the scene when I was two years old, soon after my parents' divorce. I stayed with her and my father for holidays and weekends and summers, and Kaui would open my bag—packed by my mother—and pull out a couple of shirts, a man's sock, a pair of pants, a hat. Unfazed,

Kaui always saw the strange assortment as an opportunity to go shopping, and she'd return me in my new matching jumper and a ribbon in my neatly combed hair.

Years later, as a lifestyle editor for *The Maui News*, Kaui wrote about chefs' tables at five-star resorts and attended all of the cultural events on the island. As I grew older, to my infinite delight, she often took me along. Even though she was raised during the same time as my mother, Kaui didn't see a neat house as an emblem of oppression: On the contrary, I imagine it represented power and control. Her house was immaculate, even the stuff behind closed doors, where her towels and linens lay color-coded and perfectly folded, like tidy books on a shelf. She stored miscellaneous items in pretty baskets with lids. This was wondrous to me.

My mother's closets, in contrast, were so crammed you'd have to shove it all in with one hand, slam the door with the other, then heave yourself against it and pray. The contrast between the two women applied to everything: cars, jewelry boxes, purses, countertops—and eventually, in some ways to the men they married.

YEARS AGO I went to Hawaii to promote my first book. My mother came along, and one afternoon, Kaui took us to the beach. This in itself was a surprise, because she's not an outdoorsy person. In the backseat of Kaui's Jaguar, I marveled at the smooth ride and listened as my mother told Kaui about her latest winter camping trip in Arizona.

"You know how we did dishes?" My mom paused for effect. "We rubbed sand in them."

Silence.

"It's like castaways," Kaui offered, eyes widening.

"One night it dropped down to twenty degrees. And one morning we woke up and were so excited to see fox tracks around the tent."

"Fox tracks!" Kaui let out a hoot.

"Have you heard of debris huts?" my mother asked. "They're great to know how to build if you're ever lost in the woods."

Kaui smiled, and I did, too, imagining her thoughts: *Lost in the woods? Are you kidding?*

"Yeah," my mom continued. "You burn sage to smoke out the bugs, then crawl in and pull pine boughs over you."

She glanced at Kaui to check her reaction, then we all burst out laughing.

As a young woman I was attracted to clothes and makeup, and because Kaui had two sons, I was the lucky recipient of her cast-off lipsticks and clothes and shiny purses. She took me to the best restaurants and taught me to appreciate a nice table, a beautifully presented dish. It seemed effortless, her simple, elegant approach to life. One of her homes was even featured in *Architectural Digest*.

Yet despite being forever welcome, I've always been intimi-
dated by her world. Like Gretel, I felt as if I betrayed my presence and path through her house, leaving dust, footprints, crooked
couch pillows like a trail of breadcrumbs. Still, one day, I used to
tell myself, I'll have a home like this.

AT THE BEACH we staked out our spot. Kaui brought all the gear:
bright, fluffy beach towels, chairs, mats, sunblock, magazines. She
lounged in her Donna Karan shades and cute black baseball cap;
the sand fell in Zen-ish patterns around her pedicured toes.

Beside us, squinting because she'd forgotten her sunglasses,
Mom relaxed for exactly six minutes and twenty-three seconds before needing to move again. She marched off for a walk down the
beach with a sunny "See you later!" and I watched her go, torn,
part of me wanting to join her, part of me wanting to stay.

Sometime later, Mom returned with an armful of loot: mynah
bird feathers, shells, two hairy coconuts she spied floating in the
ocean, which she had to swim out to retrieve. Kaui anxiously eyed
the wet and sandy things, probably imagining her spotless car, and
declared, "We'll have to get you a big ziplock baggie for all your
goodies!"

This brought up the story of the last time my mom hauled
back stuff from a beach trip—that time it was seaweed from a
beach in Santa Cruz, California, which she'd heard was great
for the garden. We caused quite a scene at the San Jose airport,
when Airport Security descended on us, suspicious of the terrible

smell. Mom's bag was searched for evidence of biological weapons. Kaui had tears in her eyes as we all cracked up while Mom added more funny details to the story. I realized she was proud of her adventures, and that I was too. Time spent with her is never boring.

IF KAUI BRINGS out my intimidation, my mother is the prime recipient of my frustration. If she could get more organized, her life would be easier. Filing systems! Clutter-free drawers! The peace of an orderly purse! But to her, such activities must have interfered with her more important pursuits: camping, climbing mountains, photography, writing screenplays. Her projects sprouted in piles around the house, some engulfed by passion, others left to gather dust.

Kaui's seamless order was forever out of my mother's, and my, reach. Still, I kept trying to mold mom into what I thought she should be. Why was closing a cabinet door so hard? What I never asked myself: Why was it so important to me?

Even Kaui appreciated my mother more readily than I. She always thought my mother charming, her life more relaxing. "You don't have to worry about ruining or disturbing anything," she said once. "It's about letting go."

And isn't that what I do to myself? Chastise my lack of keeping the refrigerator's bottom drawer clean versus celebrating my commitment to building fires? It seems I need to accept both of our ranges.

WHEN MY FATHER died in 2000 each woman, each a mother of one of his children, called and comforted one another. And both helped me in her own way to live without the man who'd brought us all together. I think they're more alike than I ever gave them credit for, as if both could see past the surface of things, where I could not. One prefers a B&B, one would rather sleep in a snow cave: but both measure life against priorities of the heart.

Though each has historically struggled, each is now at peace with herself, happily married for decades, living as they always meant to live. Their lives have unfurled in front of me like brightly colored carpeted rooms.

THAT DAY AT the beach we all swam in the ocean. As I watched the two of them in the water I caught my breath. The women who come before us: They toss, and at times hurl, their lessons at us, often when we're not looking—and more often before we're ready to see. If we're smart, and lucky, we open our eyes and learn what we can.

CHAPTER 28

Three Degrees at Dawn

While most songbirds we see in the summer depart for the south each fall, the chickadees are year-round residents in the north. It is remarkable that such a small bird can endure our long, cold winters. At times the difference between its core body temperature and the air temperature just outside of its feathers can be 150°F.

—Alaska Department of Fish and Game, "Chickadees"

THREE DEGREES AT dawn. Icy, invisible air seeps in through cracks in the sills and around the doors as a cup of coffee warms my hands. When I open the door to throw birdseed on the porch, the air is like something I can bite.

The cats, though restless, won't go outside, and glare at the birds from inside the sliding glass door. I go beyond the call of duty and set up a chair and some cat beds in front of the door. *Hey, cats, it's the Blue Jay Show.* Within a minute the felines have taken their seats, staring at the feeding birds like a row of kids watching cartoons. It's a rather ridiculous scene, and it reminds me of something Annie Dillard wrote in *Pilgrim at Tinker Creek*: "I find it hard to see anything about a bird that it does not want seen. It demands my full attention."

Around here, these cold snaps come through a few times each winter. This last one, days long now, has broken several "severe weather" records. Pipes are freezing all over town. Cars, sealed in frozen snow, resemble little abandoned spaceships. Deadly ice covers all four miles of Diamond Fall Road, glittering in the headlights like a path of shattered glass.

This morning, I can't get warm, though I pile on layer after layer of fleece and flannel; even a knit hat sits over my ears. I look like a homeless person and feel like a sausage. Some people tolerate cold very well; that's not been my experience. Maybe it was being half-raised in Hawaii, but I find cold to be an almost painful sensation. I'm never happier, or feel freer, than when I'm wearing a sundress and flip-flops.

Where is the sun? For six months straight, or so it seemed, each morning sunlight streamed like water into our house, through the picture windows and kitchen window and glass door. Light, and warmth. Time to make a fire, and bake something to get the oven heat as well. It occurs to me that if I took a brisk walk, it might warm me up. But I'm too cold, and lazy, to venture out. What I really need is the benefit of body heat.

Last week, when the cold came, I draped blankets over the bedroom windows and ever since have prayed the power doesn't go out. When it does, of course there's no warning, just a sudden plunge into silent darkness, as if God has finally pulled the plug on the world. When Dylan's with me, we make a fire, push the couch up close, wrap Pop-Tarts in tinfoil and tuck them in the coals.

It's harder when I'm alone.

The sadness of being without my child hasn't faded. I thought it would, that over the months I'd adjust to the rhythm of having him half the week. He calls sometimes, to tell me about a special rock he's found, or to describe what he's having for lunch. He asks what I'm doing. "Working" is my answer. I tell him I love him to the end of the world. He replies, "That's a lot of love."

These calls help, though often after we hang up, the silence, like a strong current, pulls me under. There is no resisting.

At times I feel like the shore of an ocean, and my son fills my days like a high tide, covering the contours of my life with his presence and voice, with the ever-present love and needs of a small child. When he leaves, I'm strewn with the remnants of that presence, emptied and laid bare. Along this cold shore I have learned to step carefully.

The start of winter is still a month away.

CHAPTER 29

Cabin Fever

Meadow voles, when overcrowded, turn hostile and aggressive, and eventually if conditions persist, will disperse.

—John Belden, "Agonistic Behavior in Meadow Voles"

A T 6:10 THIS morning a suspicious smell woke me up. Jimmy B has lately been missing the edge of the litter box, so the pile just sits on the floor until I get to it. Obviously, this is some kind of statement. Then, on the way to the kitchen, I stepped in a biscuity mound of khaki-colored vomit; the new food I've bought must disagree with someone, probably Cleo, who has a sensitive stomach.

It's freezing, pitch-black outside, and I'm baggy-eyed tired. Although I'm craving a cup of coffee, there are messes to clean up and five felines are impatiently waiting for breakfast. Meowing, hissing at each other, funneling through my footsteps. Oh my God: I am that crazy cat lady.

Yet these incidents are new. At first I had only three cats here, so I could handle the load easily. Then I acquired the new cats—one-eyed Jimmy B and later a bossy calico foisted on me by Bonnie (who has about twelve cats). During the rest of the year they spend much of their time, and do much of their business, outside. But winter's cold has made it necessary to lock them in around eight every night. If I don't, gaps in the cat door usher in deadly cold drafts, and besides, Max sometimes gets into fights late at night (one bad enough to require an overnight at the animal hospital).

So, sadly for all of us, the cats got a curfew.

ALL I WANT to do is write, but there's maybe twenty minutes left until Dylan wakes up and the pages are put away until tomorrow at the soonest (I've never been a late-night writer—too exhausted, my brain too jammed with the day). What will we do this morning? I'm about out of craft ideas, Dylan's bored with his books, and we recently discovered that every one of his toys is missing an essential part. It won't be remotely warm enough to venture outside until at least ten. I think to bake something before discovering we're out of eggs.

In the next instant, the power vanishes, and I'm standing in a dark kitchen.

As I place the kindling in the fireplace, Emma comes to mind. Didn't she, as a young woman, kneel in precisely this way and hold sticks of wood just like these while her children slept? Didn't she feel the same press of winter against the four walls and hear the cold wind through the trees, wind that slipped through crevices and gaps around the door? Did she feel the same weight of the need to create another day? The decades between us elide, and my actions—so ordinary and necessary—overlay upon hers, creating a palimpsest of memories. At this moment I feel closer to her than ever before.

This is winter in the forest, and I take solace in knowing it's nothing new.

YET A STRANGE thing did happen last night. Before I could lock the cat door, the cats brought in two bats. Usually the cats find mice or lizards, toting their flailing victims in their mouths and letting them free once in the house. Then the hunt is on: They stock their own private game reserve. I do my best to save these creatures (fretting more over the lizards than the mice) and am successful about half the time. It was odd to see bats, which should be hibernating by now.

The first bat didn't look like he'd make it. He crouched on the carpet, resembling a large, furred walnut. The other flew in wild circles around the room like a remote-control airplane. What a sight—those dark jagged wings whizzing by. Below, five cats prowled and scurried, darting around with tails aloft, like little sharks in a shallow pond. I bent to the grounded bat. It was the first time I'd seen one at rest, outside of one of Dylan's nature books.

This close, a bat is nothing like a bird, which to me appear alien, dinosaurish. Bats have familiar faces with little noses and mouths. He was watching me with tiny eyes, shiny as flaxseed, and his body was covered in silky black fur. As we stared at each other, I felt appraised by this bat in the way one mammal recognizes another. *Yes, I see you.*

Then, with infinite slowness, he extended his wings, an origamic unfolding of almost transparent membrane, traced with five delicate finger bones. From tip to tip he was about six inches. There he was, a miracle on my living room floor: a flying animal. (For a moment I imagined my cats spreading out long, paper wings and taking flight—a lethal thought.) Looking closer, I saw the poor bat's wings had small rips. I fought back tears as I picked him up, so carefully, and he held to my palm with the tiny hooks of his claws that enable him to climb walls and hang upside down. They felt like tiny rose thorns.

I tucked him into a cat carrier for the time being.

Then I opened the sliding glass door as wide as possible, losing all the precious heat, but the other bat would not fly out. What about echolocation? They're supposed to find openings by use of sound waves and can sense the presence of something as small as a human hair. Yet he flew by the door again and again. I began to think the bat was looking for his (or her?) friend, that he was circling the forest house, unwilling to abandon his mate.

He must have tired, because he finally landed on the wall and didn't move even when I came close, clamping a large plastic bowl over him, then easing it off the wall into the cat carrier with the other one. After locking the cat door, so the cats couldn't get out, I put the carrier, door open, on top of the far woodpile—figuring the injured one, if he could fly at all, would need some height from which to launch. Or maybe, they would crawl deep into the woodpile and rest there.

I stood in the dark for a while, but it was so cold.

I was a useless human: I had no other choice but to wish them good luck and go back inside to the comfort of the house.

The whole ordeal had taken about forty minutes, leaving the house bitterly cold and my cats wholly frustrated. Still, while the bat encounter thrilled me in some unforgettable, profound way, it came at the price of an injured animal, who might not survive.

WHEN DYLAN WAKES up I tell him about the bats and we go out to check the carrier on the woodpile. It's empty, which disappoints Dylan and relieves me. Maybe they're tucked away, safe and warm, which is as far as I let my mind drift. To distract Dylan I tell him that even though we're stuck inside because of the cold, and there aren't any kids out here to play with, and it'll be dark by five o'clock, at least we have an important project to do.

"What is it, Mama?"

"Something to keep the cats busy at night."

"Why?"

"Well, mostly so Mama doesn't go crazy."

TOGETHER WE MAKE a list of things to buy:

· cat scratch pads
· catnip
· cat treats
· cat laser toy
· Ping-Pong balls
· yarn

And we start our day.

CHAPTER 30

The Gift of Snow Geese

It is warm behind the driftwood now, for the wind has gone with the geese. So would I—if I were the wind.

—ALDO LEOPOLD, *A SAND COUNTY ALMANAC*

TODAY WOULD HAVE been my wedding anniversary. I'm alone with a stack of papers and several animals. The fire burns steadily and snows falls lightly.

Ours had been a small and lovely December wedding, the Vets Hall transformed into a winter wonderland. The rented Christmas trees were strung with twinkling white lights, and pots of lush poinsettias splashed warm color all over the room.

Kaui flew in from Hawaii, and at one point we put on a Hawaiian song. She slipped off her shoes and to everyone's amazement began to dance a hula. Kaui had begun dancing at the age of four on a sugar plantation on Maui. That night of the wedding, she was in her early sixties, but as she danced, she was transformed into a young, fluid figure. How strange and lovely—that island dance in a snowy mountain town. She brought my childhood into the room, and with it, warm waves of memories of my father and brother, of the ocean and rustle of palms.

And now inexplicably my mind jumps to a recent November afternoon, when hundreds of snow geese soared overhead, flying west, away from the winter. For days Dylan and I had seen them as we drove back and forth to town, ambling across the ranch pastures like a band of fat-bodied explorers.

That November day they were flying high above the forest house, and I don't know what brought me outside in the cold. I stood there, suddenly overcome by the glorious vision, breath caught in my chest and tears stinging my eyes. Their cries echoed over the mountain, and they flew in constantly changing patterns, as if forming and reforming the letters of words.

SOMETIMES GIFTS COME in the form of watching life, of knowing movement will happen. Kaui's hula dance showed us the grace of muscle memory, of knowing I don't need to be scared of forgetting. The snow geese's flight dared me to continue looking up and out. And I have. Or I try to.

CHAPTER 31

Blessings

*Unlike wolves, coyotes do not run in packs. They tend to hunt alone . . .
and remain active all winter, digging out rodents, capturing birds,
subsisting on available vegetation. They may hole up for a spell during bad weather.*

—STEPHEN WHITNEY, *A SIERRA CLUB NATURALIST'S GUIDE TO
THE SIERRA NEVADA*

Y OU CAN'T HOLD a child back on Christmas Day. I should
have been at his dad's at six in the morning, not six forty-
five, should have been there at five, waiting on the couch so I could
see his face as he burst into the living room. How many more
Christmas mornings will I have with him, when he's young and
it's still magical? Will he even believe in Santa next year, when it's
"my turn" with him?

By eight thirty in the morning they were gone to see relatives
over the mountains and wouldn't be back until the next evening. I

drove blindly to my brother's and stumbled up the walk and into the house, and he caught me there, while I cried against his chest, and the sounds of children swirled around us like wild joyful birds.

Later his wife—my new sister—fed me breakfast. I watched her gently shape the morning, with music and food, so that the whole house felt like a warm gift. After so many lost years, my brother has a family.

Soon we were sharing humorous stories about past holidays—funny enough to actually make me laugh, something I didn't think I'd be able to do. I even told a few, thanks to my brother's memory. All the more reason why it's good to know someone who knew you when you were young.

We exchanged gifts and watched the dogs play. Too soon, it was time to leave. For maybe the first time ever, I wasn't ready to retreat to the forest house. I stayed in town, driving aimlessly through the hushed neighborhoods, eventually going to the coffee shop, which was mercifully open, and sat with a cup of tea. I had no idea where to go.

I'll live through this day by imagining my son's, telling myself: *Dylan will be too busy to miss me. He'll be having too much fun to think of me. He's surrounded by loving family and won't notice that, once again, I'm not there.* When counting my blessings this long day, and this long night, I recite these lines first.

Merry Christmas, Son. I've given you a gift you didn't want, and shouldn't need—at least not for a very long time. I've taught you how to live without me.

CHAPTER 32

Future Tense

The California tree cricket makes a sound like a continuous trilling.
During mating season, often several males in the vicinity make the
same sound, giving a stereophonic effect. In darkness the male courts
the female with song. The female nudges the male until he stops singing.

—FIELD GUIDE TO NORTH AMERICAN INSECTS AND SPIDERS

S O I'M TWICE divorced. A divorcée x 2. Once bitten, twice
shy, so twice bitten makes me . . . thrice shy? Or is it "to the
fourth"? I was never good at math, especially algebra, and those
midget numbers above the regular numbers—exponents?—always
made me feel like I had cotton for brain matter.

A bit of research uncovers a possibly relevant term called "ex-
ponential decay." As far as I can tell, it's a formula for measuring
the rate of decay. In its simplest form, this is expressed mathemati-
cally as $y = a(1 - r)t$. Whereas a = initial amount; r = decay rate; (1
- r) = decay factor; t = time. It's usually applied to tax calculations.

Can you plug a person, a life, a relationship, into those variables?

Better keep to what I know—literary terms, like allusion and metaphor and imagery. So I find myself saying, "I'd rather stick my arm in a garbage disposal than get married again." Or, "I'd rather have a raccoon chew my face off than get married again."

These musings on the future are partly the reason why when buying a bed last spring, I selected a single. I picked one up at Susanville Discount Furniture, run by another wonderfully discreet storeowner named Peggy. My brother drove the bed to the forest house to save me the $20 delivery fee and helped me haul it into the bedroom. The bed is surprisingly tall, even throne-ish, and best of all, the mattress comes with an extra puffy layer on top. My friend Jordan gave me a queen-size burgundy velvet bedspread she'd grown tired of. This bedspread, which spills onto the floor, periodically gives me the odd feeling that I'm bedding down in a very long glass of red wine.

On the colder nights, several cats settle on the bed, anchoring me at ankles, knees, and hips, so that I may as well be swaddled in a sleeping bag. Sometimes one begins to purr, then another, then all three are going, like idling motors. My bed is a feline parking lot. Off! A few kicks and cats go flying. But in the morning, they're always back, and I emerge as if shedding a cocoon.

FOR A LONG while this small bed made me feel secure, especially those first three months when I basically slept in the fetal position. When your world closes in, it's time to burrow in even more. You don't want to stretch out, to touch that emptiness, to be reminded of a cold, alien expanse.

Lately though, the look of my bed is bothersome. The height seems to emphasize its overall smallness, its narrowness. Once, passing through the room, I was struck by the terrible image of a large, cozy coffin. By what formula, what mechanism, does comfort become confinement? Is there an equation for it? The last time I had a single bed was my junior year in college. I've been feeling the need to stretch out a bit more.

And one day, maybe in late summer, I may meet a man, a younger man with a motorcycle and no children, and he could take me on long, fast rides down two-lane highways on hot afternoons. On those rides I might close my eyes as the world rushes over and around us like a storm and I would think I'd never been so close to dying. I would be scared, would need to pull courage from somewhere inside like a rope from deep water, hand over fist.

Then I'd relax into it, the smells coming at us in waves—the hay and alfalfa and sage, the smell of cooking as we pass a farmhouse, and there would be nothing else but the sound of the wind and the engine beneath us, nothing but the feel of his body as we shoot into the sky ahead. There would be no words, no questions, just motion and release, but I'd have to be careful of the feeling that I couldn't get enough of it, that the wanting would take over my senses.

And if with him my taste for pleasure came back, my life as a mother would forever change, would divide and open, like a canyon I'd somehow have to cross.

CHAPTER 33

New Year's Day

Maybe the hardest notion to accept about winter is that it is so alive.
Beneath the bark of the leafless tree, under the frozen moss, in all the
little crevices of winter, there is life!

—*LIFE IN THE COLD: AN INTRODUCTION TO WINTER ECOLOGY*
  BY PETER J. MARCHAND (1996)

A T DAWN THIS morning, a beaded curtain of snow fell lightly
down the silvery sky. I looked out onto the porch, and a
shiny blue jay sat in the oak tree, like a leftover Christmas orna-
ment. As usual he was staring at our door with all the patience in
the world, like a little round person resting on a park bench, oblivi-
ous to the start of a new year.

It's so wonderful that the blue jays are still here. Most birds,
along with the frogs, crickets, bats, and lizards, took off a long
time ago. As if saving their energy, the blue jays are much quieter in the winter. What they are is hungry. Fortunately for them,

Dylan and I are way past throwing leftovers on the porch; each morning we spread out a feast of birdseed, cracked corn, peanuts, and suet. We are pros.

The chickadees, juncos, and nuthatches must have gotten word, because they've joined the blue jays. Dylan loves the chickadees best—they're a third of the size of the jay, their bodies dark on top and creamy white underneath, and at first glance they remind me of Dylan's tiny killer whale toys. It's Saturday, which means Dylan is with his dad, and the whale toys make me do a quick catalog of his things. The tide of his books and clothes and toys constantly washes up on the shore of either house, and at times it's hard to keep track of them all.

So here I am, at the brink of a new year. I'm warm, even if the fire is small to save wood, and I miss my child. But there's a cat in my lap and a dog at my feet, and Dylan is safe and happy. A notebook lies in front of me, a good pen. Soon I'll take a walk down the hill and look for tracks in the snow. I've gotten good at telling the difference between rabbit and raccoon, dog and fox. Yesterday a path of three-toed wild turkey tracks—like tridents stamped into the snow—wandered up the driveway and disappeared, leaving a wonderful mystery. What awaits me today, the first day of a new year?

I love that line from Mary Oliver: "Tell me, what is it you plan to do with your one wild and precious life?"

The answer is, I don't know yet. Or it's happening right now.

CHAPTER 34

Susanna on the Ice

Curlleaf mountain-mahogany wood is dry and extremely hard; it burns for a long time and produces a hot fire, thus making it, when available, a favorite fuel. Despite the hardness of the wood, the branches are brittle and snap off when submitted to strain.

—U.S. Forest Service, *Range Plant Handbook*

U NLIKE MOST PLAYDATES, this one was spur-of-the-moment. Susanna, who was coming home from an errand with her three-year-old daughter, gave me a call. Although we'd tried many times to have a playdate here, it had never worked out. This hadn't bothered me so much because Susanna is one of those housewives who, unlike me, runs a tight ship. It was better to go to her house, where I could sit on her comfortable couch and pretend to be a together sort of mom.

When she called, the kitty litter box needed attention, the sink was brimming with breakfast dishes, and the vacuum hadn't been out in three weeks. Also, Dylan and I were still in our pajamas (at noon). But I said sure because what the hell, and I lit an orange country spice candle to give the place a homey aroma. Then, as if I'd sprouted wings in the shape of dustpans, I flew around the house, wiping and washing and shoving things under the bed and into the closet. I had ten minutes, max. Dylan chased the dog. A new version of fun.

The phone rang.

"Okay, I'm on Diamond Fall Road? Where are you?"

I told her to keep going for four miles, take a right up into the forest after the last bend, then call me from there so I could direct her the rest of the way.

Ten minutes later the phone rang again.

"Joelle—we're stuck. We're slipping on the ice—my car's on the edge of a cliff! Help—I'm freaking out!"

"Okay, remain calm," I said. She sounded really panicked. "We'll be right down. Don't worry. Just stay put. It'll be fine."

I caught Dylan by the shirttail as he rounded the corner.

"Okay, Dylan, we have to rescue Susanna and Sandi. They're stuck on the ice. Right now let's go."

"Like Diego?"

"Yes—like Diego, except they're people."

We were referring to his favorite show, *Go, Diego, Go!*—a heart-racing program about an animal rescuer, wonderful in every way except Diego *SHOUTS! EVERY! SINGLE! LINE!*

"Okay, Mama."

I paused to call my neighbor Carla, who agreed to come up with her pickup truck and help. Dylan and I threw on our coats and boots and ran out the door and straight down the hill, not bothering with the road. I was thinking, *Well that's that. She'll never come here again. One by one my friends are going to cross me off their list.* I pictured Susanna in mom-loungewear (standard playdate attire), gripping the steering wheel while her terrified toddler sat in the backseat, strapped in paratrooper-style, clutching a fuzzy stuffed animal to her chest.

Meanwhile Dylan was ahead of me, hurtling down the snowy hill, through the trees, hooting like a wild animal. We scrambled to the road, headed down and round the corner, and there was Susanna's SUV parked calmly in the middle of the road. It was green and matched the trees. From inside Susanna stared at me wide-eyed and white-faced.

"*Al rescate, amigos!*" shouted Dylan. Hatless, coat flapping open, face peanut butter smeared—he looked like a feral child who'd burst out of the wilderness. But at least he was having a great time.

"Hey! We're here!" I slid and skated down to her van, remembering weeks before when my car beached like a whale on an ice berm, and the ninety terrible minutes of trying to shovel it out until finally surrendering to call my ex in humiliation. The current situation was not bad at all, because she wasn't stuck. She just needed to back straight down to the bottom of the hill, back to Diamond Fall Road. There she could get a ride with Carla, who was on her way, or walk up, or just say screw it and go home. I'd had to do this very routine a few times by now, when I couldn't make it up. I'd even done it with Dylan; it's a drag, because you have to walk up a long way with a small child in the cold, and maybe a bag of groceries, and your car might end up buried in the snow by morning—but it's not actually life threatening.

I peered in the passenger window at my normally confident friend.

"I'm going to vomit," she said, and clapped a hand to her mouth.

Behind us, Dylan whooped like the boy from *The Jungle Book*. Susanna gaped at him and revealed the first glimmer of a smile. How can you worry when a four-year-old is dancing with joy?

"I'm petrified that the van is going to slip off the side and into a tree."

"It's under control, really. It'll be fine," I said, and tried to look reassuring.

That was me, I suddenly realized, looking at her paralyzed with worry, at her attempt to be brave and not show her child how scared she really was. Last winter I'd felt the same fear, had been frozen in the same place. I thought of the Winnie the Pooh book I'd read to Dylan a hundred times, when Christopher Robin tells Pooh: "You're stronger than you think, and braver than you know."

I checked out Sandi in the backseat, nestled in her puffy pink coat. She gazed at me blithely. She had nothing to worry about, with her supermom in the front seat. Just then a pickup truck turned onto the road and started up toward us. It was Bonnie, who'd been visiting Carla.

"See—here comes my neighbor."

Bonnie parked, and she and Carla got out, wearing sturdy boots and thick canvas jackets. They strode across the ice, looking like pioneer women who could chop down a tree with a dull ax. *How cool*, I thought, *women to the rescue*.

THE PLAN WAS simple: After Susanna and her daughter got out of the van, Bonnie backed it down to the bottom, parked it, then hiked up. She was going to drive us all in the pickup to my house. Susanna and Sandi got in the cab; Carla, Dylan, and I climbed into the back of the truck. We held on tight as Bonnie drove up the road, the icy wind blowing back our hair. It felt glorious—I was free and hadn't even known it.

"Whee!" Dylan shouted. Carla and I laughed, and the truck bounced and skidded up the road to the forest house.

We ended up having a great time, that day, and Susanna and I laughed like children. How grateful I am to have friends like her. Later I thought again of that story, when Pooh and his friends overcome their fears to help someone else. Maybe it's only when we have to save someone else that we finally understand we can take care of ourselves.

CHAPTER 35

Cliffs and Clouds

The tolerance of California black oak to shade varies . . . The need for top light increases as the tree ages. In dense stands, black oak often fills a "hole" in the canopy, sometimes leaning 15 to 20 degrees to do so. If overtopped, the oak either dies outright or dies back successively each year.

—U.S. Forest Service, "California Black Oak"

THERE'S A BIG bash this weekend. It's Kim's I CAN'T BELIEVE I'M FORTY party. It'll be held at a local pool hall/bar, and she's hired a DJ and his karaoke machine. The place will be decorated in red, with red roses and plates and an enormous cake. Over a hundred people are invited.

Kim's the first of my mom friends to crash into the forty milestone, which I'd already stumbled over. I was a new mother at the time, so turning that pivotal age didn't register much. I felt plump and distracted, and the idea of aging floated like the distant clouds

on the Diamonds. Between then and now, though, those clouds
have swelled and begun to loom, ever so slightly.

Kim's is the first party I will have gone to since moving into
the forest house, which means I haven't gone out with my friends,
aside from playdates and coffee, for a year. It's the kind of event
I used to love when I was younger, anticipating it for weeks, and
often buying a new outfit. Now it's hard to remember what all
the fuss is about. I'm not looking to meet a guy, and being one of
the older guests there tinges my anticipation with nostalgia, the
sad kind.

It doesn't help that the party is at a bar, the type of establish-
ment that's all about drinking and getting laid. I haven't felt like
going to a place like this in at least a decade. There will probably
be—awful thought—dozens of people young enough to be my children. I get the weird feeling that at this party I'll be going out with
my former self: "New me, meet the formerly younger me."

Admittedly, I don't look bad for my age. Oh—should that qual-
ifier be put in parentheses (for my age), or in quotes, "for my age,"
or in italics, *for my age*? Is it bitterness I feel, or irony, or pride, or
outrage? Who can say, when the feeling changes all the time?

FOR A COUPLE of years now, something has happened to my
face—specifically around my nose. Little capillaries have emerged
and, like tiny red alfalfa sprouts, spread and began to bloom.
An awful garden has taken root in my face. Makeup worked for
a while, but then it had to be reapplied about ten times a day.

Without concealer, I looked like I'd just had a good cry, or was suffering from allergies. On cold days, I resembled one of those alcoholic gamblers parked at a Reno slot machine.

As the tender roots reached further and further, I imagined my cheeks crisscrossed with hairlike red lines—eventually I'd have the map of Oakland, California, on my face.

Bottom line: Those migrating veins were making me look, and feel, old. You never see young people with this problem. I've seen twenty-five-year-olds with crow's feet, but not broken capillaries. *Why me?* I thought. Other forty-somethings didn't seem to have this issue. Finally, I saw an aesthetician, who said it could have something to do with the blood disorder I'd been diagnosed with after a miscarriage. When I finally became pregnant, I needed to inject the drug heparin into my stomach twice a day for the duration of the pregnancy. So maybe I don't have the best veins.

A facialist told me I'd look ten years younger if my nose were "zapped." Zapping doesn't sound so bad. I drove the two hours to Reno, where most medical things are done. I lay down on a bed in a very clean medical "spa" room, and white-coated Darcy painted cold, gooey gel around my nose. Then she placed little plastic eye goggles over my eyes. They felt like grapes. I could feel her peering at my face, her wafting breath sterile and faintly minty.

"Hmm. Unfortunately you have quite a few collapsed capillaries *inside* your nostril and they're really noticeable. The skin is thin there, so it'll hurt."

Next came some ominous rustling, and a long pause, then *Zap!* The pain, while gone in less than a second, was outrageous. Imagine a just-blown-out match (still glowing) pressed inside your nostril. There's even a burning odor.

"Okay that looks great," Darcy said. "But we'll have to do a few more passes."

God no.

To make matters worse, each burning coal zap is accompanied by a brilliant flash of light—like a floodlight flipping on right in front of your eyeballs. The grape-goggles may as well have been daubs of toilet paper. *Zap-Flash! Zap-Flash!* Each time, I flinched uncontrollably all the way down to my toes. Amazing—the body's reflexes. I could no more have resisted flinching than begun to levitate.

After fifteen minutes, it was over. I'd aged about a year. Then Darcy—who might be all of twenty-seven—made a tantalizing offer.

"Hmmm. I'm noticing some age spots," she said, drawing a soothing gloved finger around my face. "A few little bitty zaps here and there and we'll get rid of them. It'll hurt a lot less because the skin's less sensitive."

"Okay," I said, and she went to work. It wasn't as bad as my nose, but I still left feeling like I'd been scattershot by flaming grains of uncooked rice. Each time I flinched I told myself, *Younger chin! Younger cheek!*

Now I was ready, more or less, for Kim's I CAN'T BELIEVE I'M FORTY party.

I'VE ALWAYS HAD a fear of jumping off cliffs into lakes or rivers. Even as others leaped off with howls of delight, it would take sometimes half an hour or more for me to gather the courage. Something about that first unknown vault over the edge kept me glued to the top. When I finally did, every time it was a blast. And I'd go up and do it again.

In the same way, I used to be afraid of turning thirty, then thirty-five; I was nauseated by the entire decade of my forties. My fifties and sixties made me weak in the knees with terror. It reminds me of something that happened with my friend Richelle, my best friend since college. We were eating appetizers at a bar of a fancy bistro in Mill Valley, California. We thought we looked pretty good, though we were both (ridiculously) sensitive about being thirty-one.

Feeling cocky, we asked the young, handsome bartender to guess our age. We smugly figured he'd say twenty-five or so. But he guessed exactly right, on the first try. He must have seen how mortified we were, because he tried to explain by saying we looked very sophisticated and professional, the way ladies in their thirties do.

I remember the dismay we felt even now—more than a decade later. That fear, even disgust, of growing older seems like such a waste now, because more and more, each time I've reached the dreaded number—like those long-ago cliffs I finally leaped off—it's not been scary at all. In some ways it's even been exhilarating.

This anticlimactic passing of the age mark has happened so many times that I've begun to believe it'll just continue. When I turn fifty-eight, for example, I'm willing to bet there will be a lot to like about being that age. There'll be other priorities to consider. And I trust I'll be healthy. I'll have a son, and friends and family, and dreams fulfilled, or at least taking shape.

As the gaze shifts backward now, at younger people—twenty-four, thirty-four, even thirty-nine—I remember how confused I was, how low my confidence, how quickly I suppressed myself to please others. I've begun to look, not with envy, but with fond sympathy, at younger women. There were plenty of them at Kim's party—which was great fun after all—and I smiled at them, wishing them the best. What else can I do?

There's a famous quote from a May Sarton poem: "Now I become myself. It's taken / Time, many years and places." I love that quote, the way it reminds us to honor the past, and to enjoy our lives, right now, while we can.

CHAPTER 36

The Peppermill

*The caterpillar of the swallowtail butterfly, like most caterpillars,
feeds on the foliage of trees. Some overwinter partially grown and
pupate in loose cocoons hidden among fallen leaves.*

—*Field Guide to North American Insects and Spiders*

I HELD ON TIGHT as we rose, ever so slowly, sixty-five feet in the air—as tall as the ponderosas back home outside the forest house. Dylan and I were riding on the Ferris wheel inside Scheels, a mega–sports store in Reno. We'd paid a dollar to risk our lives, strapped in only by a simple piece of cloth. If we leaned forward we'd pitch headlong to the floor dozens of feet below. When was the last time I'd ridden a Ferris wheel? Thirty years ago?

"Don't be scared," I whispered, mostly to myself.

"This is so fun, Mama!" Dylan shouted.

I couldn't believe Dylan wasn't bleating in fear. He must get his bravery from his dad.

By the way, this heart-in-your-throat experience was Susanna's idea. On the way to Reno for our mother-son adventure, I called her for advice on what to do. She rattled off a list of kid-friendly restaurants and stores.

"Oh, and there's this great Ferris wheel at Scheels!" she said, never mentioning it was full-size.

Finally the ride was over, and after purchasing a couple of toys, we grabbed lunch and headed for our ultimate destination, the Peppermill hotel and casino.

At the Peppermill, two things were constantly on my mind. First was Dylan's safety: I was on constant orange-alert. Far from our comfort zone of the quiet forest house and our small town, I held onto Dylan's hand as if we'd been welded together. Even though the Peppermill is considered the most family-friendly of the hotel-casinos—and it's miles away from the snarl and gritty action of downtown Reno—it's still a casino.

In his life, I've only lost track of Dylan twice, and both times, during those approximately two to three minutes, my heart caught on fire and plunged into my gut. Both times, the innocent surroundings turned sinister, like a movie scene fading to black. The memories will likely never leave; I can still recall that piercing terror, knowing my life might end if I didn't find him.

The first time he disappeared, he was two and a half, and we were in Hawaii, on our way from the car to a beachfront condo.

While I was getting our bags out of the car, he'd followed my step-dad down the path to the condo. He was safe in Doug's care the whole time. But I didn't know that—in my mind, my son was gone.

The other time, we were in Walmart, and Dylan took off with his cousin around the next aisle—and from there they vanished. In each of these incidents I had family with me. At Walmart, my mother and I split up to find the kids. In Hawaii, my stepmother and I did the same thing. The presence of family offered at least a shred of consolation. But this time in Reno, I was alone, and the fact never left my consciousness.

The second thing hovering over my mind was my father. I didn't expect him to be there, though I should have known. He loved gambling, and casinos. For many years, on their anniversary, he and my stepmom Mimi flew from Maui to Reno, where they mostly gambled and partied and had a great time.

My father died ten years ago, almost to the day. He was fifty-nine years old and never got to meet any of his three grandchildren, all boys.

AT THE PEPPERMILL, we kept getting lost. The skywalks and stairs and elevators and "wings" make no sense. It was like that movie, *Being John Malkovich*: each hallway and doorway opened onto another portal. We weren't the only ones, by the way; others stood in front of signs and maps, scratching their heads, or wandered around with frowning faces, and we'd shrug at each other as we passed. You lost? Me too!

Beside me Dylan trundled along, caught up in the sense of purpose, the important feeling of being on a mission: Find the pool! Find the room! Find the arcade!

Meanwhile, I kept glimpsing my father's ghost. I first saw him when we were in the swimming pool, which was heated to a balmy temperature. Dylan and I sunk in the water like otters. It seemed like a dream, to be swimming outside in winter. My father looked down from a window, watching over us as Dylan and I floated in the warm water.

As I splashed with my son, my mind drifted to pleasant childhood memories of swimming with my father in Hawaii. It was in the clear blue waters of Kauai's Hanalei Bay that he taught me to swim before I could walk. For me, Hawaii was always warm, awash in tropical splendor and lush beauty, a Garden of Eden–like experience where you are face-to-face with nature all the time, even the windows of your house fitted with screens instead of glass, to let the wind breathe through the rooms.

It was also a world steeped in the culture of ʻohana, or family. During my childhood, I lived this life once or twice a year, for a few weeks, a month, and the visits always reminded me strangely of warm baths, of the experience of being dipped into a soothing embrace of water—and then when it was time to leave, of being lifted out of that embrace, as vulnerable as a wet, cold child.

Lately I've been thinking of how different my life might have been, if my mother hadn't left my father in Kauai, when I was still a baby. Not just in the obvious sense of having my parents together, but I would have been raised in Hawaii. Of course I would still be a *haole*, a word that has come to represent a Caucasian but which also means foreigner or, literally, "one without breath." Even so, I would have called the islands my home, as my father was able to do. I would not have traveled back and forth over the Pacific year after year, between the islands and California, between my father and my mother, so that I was never home on either shore, and always dreaming in one place of the other.

AFTER THE POOL, we somehow found the arcade, which appears to be a roomful of fun games, but is really a training ground for future gamblers. Here Dylan had great fun, but then it was time for dinner. I felt my father's presence most strongly when we descended to the ground floor with the restaurants and casino. Once I saw him at the poker table, wearing his familiar faded jeans and soft flannel shirt. He waved and smiled. Later he sat at the sports bar, telling a joke to the bartender and other patrons, cracking everybody up like he always used to do. He could make you feel like whatever your troubles or fears, they weren't really so bad.

I was glad he was there because it was an uncomfortable journey across a vast, foreign wilderness—the endless flow of people, cigarette smoke and liquor, clanging slot machines and blinking lights, background music verging on too loud. It was only five fifteen, but like all casinos, it always feels like midnight. I suddenly missed our town, its sense of safety, of good neighbors, and the feeling of being part of a place that has both welcomed and accepted me. I knew this feeling would stay, and I sighed relief.

We finally reached the haven of the restaurant, where we shared soup and a veggie cheeseburger. It occurred to me in a profound way that Dylan was growing up quickly, that in some ways he was already a little man, with no need of a booster seat, and doing just fine with his plate of food and towering glass of milk.

We've crossed over into new territory, and there's no going back.

AT THE PEPPERMILL things were just getting started, but for us it was time for bed. We got lost again on our way back to the room, but that was okay, just another adventure, and in the room Dylan jumped out his last few sparks of energy on the bed.

"That's your side," I said, pointing to his half, "and this is mine. See?"

He nodded. "That's right, Mama."

We settled in with three of the books we'd brought, including his favorite, *The Goodnight Gecko*. I tucked him in with his satin "lovey" blanket, which he's had since he was five months old. All around us the casino pulsed with anxious life, yet Dylan lay with me, perfectly at peace.

I'd gotten a king bed for the extra room and so I'd only have to worry about his rolling off one side. But he kept edging toward my side, legs sprawling out like a little frog prince. At one point he lay parallel to the pillows with his feet at my neck. Around four or so I gave up trying to nudge him back over and curled up in the remaining space, where I dreamed of threading through mazes of glittering palm trees and dark, green mountains.

I never told Dylan his grandfather was there, but maybe that's why he was so calm and happy the whole time at the Peppermill, even when we were lost. Maybe Dylan felt the comforting presence of a kind of angel, one he never had the chance to meet, but whose love is with us just the same.

CHAPTER 37

Overwinter

The better the root system, the better the chance the plant will survive the winter.

—Tina M. Smith, "Overwintering Containerized Perennials"

M Y MOTHER AND stepdad have moved back to town. They sold their New Mexico property and drove up here with their travel trailer and three horses. They're caretaking a few acres on the outskirts of town. It's a transition time, hunkering down for the cold months while they figure out where to go next. In wildlife biology the term is "overwinter," which means to pass through or wait out the winter season.

Sometimes Dylan and I go out to the property and hang out with them and the horses. We muck manure and spread hay around the pasture. Dylan loves the horses, and they seem endlessly curious about him, nudging and smelling his head and neck while he laughs. They're so gentle; I love the sight of his open hand, offering a slice of carrot to an enormous white muzzle and those lips reaching down like two ripe peaches.

We take a break and get a snack in Mom and Steve's trailer, which is about thirty-five feet long. They've lived here nearly six years. The kitchen is even smaller than mine, with room for only one person. Somehow they sleep in there, along with their two big dogs, Annie and Bailey, nearly horses themselves as part Labs, part Great Danes. Everything is jerry-rigged, and their battle with the dirt and cold is a full-time job. Taking a shower at their place is like standing in an upright coffin and pouring a coffee can of warmish water over your head.

It's a life they've chosen, though not many understand why. I figure comfort is relative, and at times overrated, and it's hard not to admire the way my parents tackle life's realities head-on. How many sixty-eight-year-old women get up at dawn to break up ice so a horse can have a drink of water? Now that I'm on my own, having them close by again has made it easier for me to feel a part of this town.

Lately I've been going to AA meetings with my mom once a week or so, just as I did when I was a teenager and she was newly sober. There's a noon meeting each weekday at the Fellowship Hall on Weatherlow Street. Usually about ten people attend, sometimes as many as twenty. Some of the old-timers I've known for fifteen years; others I recognize from around town.

The "newcomers" always stop me cold when they share. Some have three days of sobriety, others thirty; a few are skidding up to a year. They come to the meetings to get warm and be with people who care. Often their lives are so bad, or they're in such binds—with a parole officer maybe, or they've just lost their kids to foster care—that I leave feeling as if my own life glows in comparison.

These meetings remind me that the only antidote to depression and self-pity is gratitude. Sometimes, usually around two in the morning, I turn on my book light and get out pen and paper, and then I start listing things to be grateful for.

It's best to start with the essentials:

· My child is safe.
· I'm not in a wheelchair.
· I'm not in jail.
· I have a roof over my head.
· I have a car that runs.

IF YOU START from scratch like this, the list can go on for an hour and put you finally to peaceful sleep. And if you keep going, you work yourself up to the light:

· I am a daughter who is loved.
· I am the mother of a healthy beautiful boy.
· Spring is coming.
· Thank you.

CHAPTER 38

Where Your Life Meets the Sky

The downward rush of the golden eagle is the swiftest thing, as it is the most magnificent thing, in the bird world. Its lofty soaring flight is equally grand, as it mounts in ascending spirals up into the clouds until lost to sight.

—Arthur Cleveland Bent, *Life Histories of North American Birds of Prey*

Since I moved into the forest house, I've wanted to hike to the top of the mountain that rises behind us. For the longest time I was too afraid, because this is the kind of venture you have to notify at least two people about.

When I called my neighbor Carla to let her know my plan, she told me about the guy who lived not far down the road, who'd gone out one day to cut some wood, and a branch fell on him.

"He lay there all day, until he died, because no one knew where he was."

"Oh no," I said, horrified.

Mostly, I was afraid of mountain lions. But now I had my dog. I called a friend in town, to let her know my plans too.

"You should take someone along," she said. "Besides, I've heard dogs can actually *attract* mountain lions."

I got off the phone, tired of warnings. The whole point of this was to go by myself. It was one of those things you need to do alone, so you know you can. Also, I was inspired. I'd just read a book, *Savage Summit*, about the women who've climbed K2. A terrific read, it's also one of those ambulance-chaser books, where you know the person is going to perish, and in a bad way at that, like first losing a nose and fingers before slowly freezing to death, or being swept by blizzard winds from the mountain face and hurled into an icy crevasse.

Sure, my hike would be long and steep and would take hours, and it was the middle of winter, but this isn't exactly the Himalayas. Those women could have skipped up my mountain. Even though a part of me is quite lazy and would rather curl up on the couch with some chocolate than tackle a mountain, I wanted to be like them, to a point. I wanted to see what lay beyond the forest house.

SO ONE DAY, after two weeks of bitter cold and two days of snowfall, the sun came out, and Bella and I set off up the slope. Right away it was clear that hiking in new snow is not a great idea. However, in addition to being lazy, I'm stubborn, so onward we climbed. In half an hour I'd gone past the edge of the burn, which was the farthest I'd ever hiked. This was officially new territory. The dead trees of the Cheney Creek Fire, now covered with snow, made me think of angels. After a while we came across some deer tracks flecked with blood, with long straight lines where one hoof had dragged in the snow.

The tracks led to a melted circle, with matted grass where the deer had lain to rest. I followed the trail for a while, finding another wet, matted circle, and more blood. I kept expecting to stumble over her body. But the trail disappeared, or I lost it, and so maybe she was lucky and got away.

We kept climbing. The sun's light began to weaken, and fog and mist drifted over the Diamonds on the other side. Not a house, not a wire, a road, anywhere in sight. I knew from maps that we could have walked for ten square miles and not seen a trace of humanity. Once we crossed Highway 36, we'd have entered vast national forest land that stretches all the way to Oregon. All year I'd wanted to stand at the top and look onto the other side, to view those miles and miles of wilderness, to say *Here, I've made it* while the orchestral joy of *The Sound of Music* rose around me and epiphanies and revelations soared like eagles above.

But after an hour and a half, we were still trudging up through the snow. In places it was so steep, and the snow so soft, that I had to crawl on hands and knees. Bella, in snow to her throat, was beginning to look nervous.

The higher we climbed, the thicker the fog, until we couldn't
see the Diamonds anymore, or the edge of town eight miles out.
Suddenly I stopped, unable to go forward. It reminded me of a line
in Peter Matthiessen's *The Snow Leopard*, in which he describes an
intense moment during his trek in the mountains of Nepal: "I wait,
facing the north; instinct tells me to stand absolutely still. Cloud
mist, snow, and utter silence, utter solitude: extinction."

This ominous moment flooded me with memories of life as a
teenager on the Oregon Coast, where we'd spend hours exploring
the rocks and the tidepools that bordered the cold, surging dark
ocean. We'd breathe in that sharp sea air until we noticed the rising water, the coming tide, bringing with it that familiar unease of
the world closing in. I'd feel comforting resignation that home is
where you're supposed to be, not out here so far away, on the edge
of the world.

The fog swelled in the sky around us, limiting my view to what
was immediately around me. I could only sense the earth and trees,
forced to imagine the unknown world. Slowly I realized there was
no actual top of the mountain, just a ridge, and another beyond. In
the fog, a third ridge was just visible in the distance, like the emerging prow of a ghost ship.

At one point Bella grasped my gloved hand in her mouth, usually a sign of play, but this was different. *Let's go home*, she was
telling me. There's no orchestra here, no eagles.

I stopped. And what came to me was this: The edges that have
always ringed my life do not seem quite so close.

There was no way to know, almost a year ago, that the forest house would turn out to be a good vantage from which to view these edges, the places from which I might fall: poverty, alcoholism, despair, bad love. Some I've only brushed against; others, like despair, and bad love, I've leaped right over the cliff and tumbled into their abyss.

I had wanted to see clearly. But maybe we have to go on faith. Maybe there isn't always a clear-cut vision of the land around us, of the future, of our path through it. There's just the knowledge that whatever lies ahead, we'll be all right.

The edges of my life will probably never vanish; the horizon will always be there. The best I can hope for is that they'll continue to recede, giving me more room to live, and live well.

CHAPTER 39

The Rock Garden

Not all seeds blown in the wind will find a suitable place to grow.
Only a small proportion are likely to find the perfect position.

—ERIC A. BOURDO, *THE ILLUSTRATED BOOK OF TREES*

T HE FOREST HOUSE is for sale. It has been for a few years, so
I don't worry much. Like a slightly dangerous animal, this is
a fact from which I've kept my distance.

Sometimes, though, mainly at night, it wanders back to growl
hello. I'm reminded yet again that we'll have to move one day—but
when, and where? How could we ever match this amazing rent of
$400 a month? I've seen the local classifieds—if we moved, our
rent would double.

Like my mother, I'll likely always be at the mercy of my finances. She was a hardworking woman, limited only by the
amount of her paycheck. Hopefully I can pull off what she did: always managing to make my brother and me feel middle-class even

when we ate Crock-Pot beans and homemade bread for weeks on end; even when we needed a roommate or two to help pay the rent.

Wendell Berry asks in one of his essays, "The world is full of places. Why is it that I am here?" His question reminds me of the day I hiked the mountain behind my house—it was as if the sky had draped itself over me, like a lowered blanket. It had felt oddly protective and close, the way my life is now, here with my son and his father in this town. I have been chastened, and relieved, finally, because isn't it an ironic kind of freedom, when you embrace the landscape that is *yours* and no other, and so can move sure-footed from this day on?

So I know why I'm here, in Susanville. For my son. This is what can finally change you: a child. Mine needs to be near his father. Theirs is a bond, mysterious to me, but one for which to be forever grateful. I've seen what happens to men who grow up without the loving presence of a father. And so we will stay in this town as long as we need to, and we will be fine.

The question that haunts me more: How would we ever find another house like this, in the forest?

I imagine moving to the apartments in town, where most single parents end up, lured by convenience and cheap rent. There, roads are plowed in winter, lawns mowed in summer, etc. It's always an easy walk from the numbered parking space to the front door. My mother, often in haste, settled us into such places many times. My father, too, in between wives. If that's where Dylan and I have to go, there will be, I expect, an eerie sense of nostalgia in those rooms, with their thin walls and worn Formica, the cool softness of faded linoleum under my bare feet, always surrounded by the sounds of others who live in replicas of our rooms.

And beneath that uneasy familiarity, would there also be a kind of defeat at the knowledge that I haven't traveled very far from my parents' struggles? That I'm simply continuing a pattern of moving from place to place, a never-ending search that over time becomes an end in itself? I read somewhere we humans are the most restless of species, and that is especially true for my family. How we loved the feeling of starting over, of opportunity, of newness. How we loved the search for what I now know is simply *home*.

For the first time I don't feel that ever-present pull to move on. Now I want to, I need to, stay. The restlessness that's always shadowed me like a second skin has mostly left. Part of it must be growing older. When he was in his late twenties, Rick Bass once wrote of how "intoxicating" it was to have "nothing behind us anymore, and to have everything ahead of us." I remember feeling that way. The expanse of youth, the open road. When does it shift? When do you begin carrying something from behind? For me, that is what divorce with children is.

I've become attached to this place. To this forest. There's room for me to grow here, yes, but there's also a sense of being home.

THE WRITER SARA Maitland says people "crave" landscape. The place she craves, which is very detailed and beautiful and nothing like mine, is a "landscape of silence":

The landscape of my silence had become very clear to me.
It is high moorland: a long view across rough grass and an
unbroken line where the hill meets the sky. It is not being
tucked in under a steep mountain, or in a wood, but open
to the wind. Equally, it is not about dramatic and chal-
lenging peaks. It is a huge and silent nothing of peat bog,
rough grass, bracken, broken walls enclosing no fields and
the harsh cry of curlew on the wing.

It's the landscape of forest that calls to me. The forest is where my mother's family came from in Sweden. The landscape of my ancestors is a dense, dark wood. This is how the writer Selma Lagerlöf described the spruce forest of western Sweden: "silent and dark, bearded and pungent." Trolls lived in those woods, and bears and wolves, and within them woodsmen traveled by sleigh on snowy paths. It was a mystical world that no longer exists except, maybe, in the darkest hollows of my soul's memory.

When our family was forced to separate and leave Sweden, we all became displaced. When Emma left the Mother Country, we were forever cut off from our landscape of home. Have I, all this time, been waiting to return?

FOR ABOUT EIGHT months now, Dylan and I've been building a rock garden. He comes back to me on Sunday nights, and if the weather permits, in the morning, after breakfast, we hunt for rocks. We each take a bag and head off down the dirt road to the bottom, where it meets Diamond Fall Road, where the rocks collect at the base of the stream. We find the smoothest ones and bring them home to be washed and painted, transformed into ladybugs and turtles, flags and trucks, all vibrant splashes of color.

Then we place them at the base of the immense western juniper at the edge of the porch. When you pull up to our house you'll see dozens of brightly painted rocks, pinecones, and strips of wood ringing the tree. Some of these rocks were already there—huge rocks, dug deep into the ground. These are the anchors, and I like the feel of them, their implacable weight and strength. Their permanence. Nothing moves them, not even the most violent of storms.

In a passage about leaving a beloved place, Berry wrote that there was a "troubling sense that what we were going to would be more ordinary than what we were leaving behind. And it was." I try not to think about the fact of moving, of searching for another place to call home.

And what will become of the forest house? Who will feed the blue jays and chickadees? The deer? Who's to say what the next people will do with these rocks under the juniper tree? Maybe they'll toss them down the hill, or use them to build a fence. Over time, sun and rain will wear away the colors.

Wallace Stegner wrote that "home is what you can take away with you." I hope he is right. At least the memory of our rock garden will never fade. It will remain with us, as will the memories of the forest house. We can bring them with us, wherever we go.

ACKNOWLEDGMENTS

I may have written my pages alone in a quiet forest, but many people helped make *The Forest House* possible. Thank you to my wonderful agent, Penny Nelson, for tirelessly believing in me, and to my editor Liz Parker and all the staff at Counterpoint Press, for embracing my work and creating a beautiful book.

For his expertise, research assistance, and invaluable library, my heartfelt appreciation goes to Tom Rickman of the U.S. Forest Service. To my generous readers, my deepest thanks: Richelle Thomson, Kelly Fairbank, B.J. Ryan, and the talented folks of the Thompson Peak Writers' Group. To my "mom friends," Darryl, Leyla, Jordan, and Aura, thanks for being there.

For her exquisite illustrations that immeasurably enhanced my writing, my gratitude goes to my dear friend, Crystal Keesey.

For their constant and loving support, especially during the dark days, I am so lucky to have my family: Mom and Mark, Aunt Kathy, Kaui, Ken, Mimi, and Dace and Payton and their new family.

To Jason Colbert, a hug and kiss: you helped me more than you know.

A special thank you to my son, who, one way or another, was always with me and always will be.

© JORDAN CLARY

JOELLE FRASER is the author of *The Territory of Men: A Memoir*, and received MFAs from The University of Iowa and Eastern Washington University. A MacDowell Fellow, her award-winning work has appeared in many literary journals, including *The Iowa Review*, *Crazyhorse*, *Hawai'i Pacific Review*, and *Fourth Genre*. She lives in northeast California with her son.